W9-BYA-408

THE LITTLE LEAD SOLDIER

The LITTLE LEAD SOLDIER

WORLD WAR I LETTERS
FROM A FATHER TO HIS SON

HUGH D. WISE, III

WESTHOLME
Yardley

Facing title page: The Little Lead Soldier. (*Hugh D. Wise, III*)

Westholme Publishing, LLC
904 Edgewood Road
Yardley, Pennsylvania 19067
Visit our Web site at www.westholmepublishing.com

ISBN: 978-1-59416-274-9
Also available as an eBook.

Printed in the United States of America.

To Mary, my loving wife and best friend

CONTENTS

List of Illustrations

An unnumbered illustration gallery follows page 94

INTRODUCTION

A
S A CHILD, I KNEW THAT ON THE SHELVES OF MY parents' library was a leather-covered, bound unpublished book entitled "The Letters of a Little Lead Soldier in the World War." It was written by my grandfather, who had been a regular army colonel in World War I. He died in 1942, six weeks before I was born. Like my father, I was named for him. The book held typewritten letters from a toy soldier that had been given to the colonel by his six-year-old son, my father, who had asked the soldier to write him of his upcoming war experiences. I can only imagine what my grandfather thought of receiving such a tender and innocent request as he prepared for war.

Other than an occasional glance, I ignored the book, even though it held a hallowed status in the eyes of my parents. Perhaps I was tired of hearing about the derring-do of dead ancestors when I was trying to make my own way growing up, then through law school and as an adult. When my parents died, I selected the book as part of my inheritance. By that time, I had become interested in what Colonel Hugh Douglas Wise had to say about one of the most calamitous events of modern history.

I started by reading the typewritten letters in the book, without being aware of the importance of some handwritten letters that I had also inherited. Those had been carefully tied into packets secured together by cross-hatched string, and sometimes red ribbon. I doubt that the packets had been opened since the time when they were first read until I did so. The elaborate, ritualistic packaging suggests that the letters were to be treasured, preserved, and reread at a later time, as I have done.

Some of the packets contained handwritten Little Lead Soldier letters which my grandfather, at a later time, had typed and bound into a book. The neatly folded letters in the packets were etched with precise penmanship flowing from a fountain pen onto good stationery, quite special considering wartime limitations. The colonel's energy, through his surrogate, the Lead Soldier, surges through to the reader.

Because of the problems of sending mail from the battlegrounds, many of the letters were probably sent in batches, and some may never have been sent but were later personally delivered. I like to think of my grandmother reading out loud those that were addressed to my father. There were booms and bangs to amuse my father and his two young brothers, along with the deadly seriousness of war, hopefully beyond the comprehension of that young audience. I think that you and I were also an intended audience.

Although plenty of action, guts, and glory are recounted, especially toward the end, the letters also thoughtfully describe the beautiful French countryside and, at times, a serenity quite the opposite of the frenetic activities of battle. They show insight, imagination, and, sometimes, whimsical philosophy. They also depict the mindset of a totally dedicated warrior, bent on saving the world. He did help do so, at least for a short while.

Much has been written of the tribulations of the privates in the World War I trenches, and the lives of the generals have also been fully described by themselves and others. The colonel lived some of each style. He commanded the 61st Infantry Regiment that numbered up to five thousand soldiers; sometimes he was housed in baronial luxury, other times he slept in the trenches with his men. He was the target of gun and artillery fire, grenades, bombs, and gas. The letters are a narrative of that man's experience, which included being awarded the prestigious French Croix de Guerre for heroism.

The colonel spent much of his time in and around the picturesque French Vosges Mountains which border Germany and Switzerland. In lively style, the Lead Soldier described the Vosges trench warfare in terms of deadly games of no ultimate consequence—except to the casualties. When finally out of those trenches, he verbally sketched the large-scale battles of St. Mihiel and Meuse-Argonne with their massive brutality. The picture that he drew was more vivid than what I found in the history books that I read for background to this volume.

I became interested in what drove my grandfather to become who he was. Among the packets of letters that I inherited were those of my grandfather to and from his wife, Ida, my grandmother. The Little Lead Soldier did not tell of my grandfather's and grandmother's personal burdens. I am able to because I learned it from these intimate letters. They gave me a greater understanding of the pain that my grandfather endured, not only for the cause he fervently believed in, but also for his own fulfillment, and how my grandmother had to take care of three young sons while worrying about her husband and struggling when his salary was delayed.

I found that the Little Lead Soldier was a fickle scribe, not always reporting all that he saw or heard. I decided to put the letters into the context of what was happening outside the observation of either the Little Lead Soldier or the Colonel. In spite of setting out to be a disinterested reporter of events, I could not avoid inserting my own thoughts. I doubt that my grandfather would agree with some of those ideas. I wish that I could converse with him, but now I know some of his thoughts, as he expressed them. Mine come from hindsight and no personal experience; I was not there. I do not advocate the position that the "war to end all wars" should not have been fought. German militarism had no place in a civilized world, but I question the leadership on both sides that led to so much death in the final months of the war when the outcome had already been determined.

World War I encompassed the globe and consumed millions of young lives over five horrific years. This is the story of a little boy, his father, and a toy soldier that would see that boy's father safely home.

ONE

THE TRAIN NORTH

Allons à La France!

After years of waiting and months of anticipation, Colonel Hugh Douglas Wise began his trip to France on April 7, 1918. Eventually, he would travel to bloody Meuse-Argonne. He had been on many train rides, but this ride was not routine. "Here" was Camp Greene, North Carolina; "there" was Fort Merritt, New Jersey, close to New York City and the embarkation port of Hoboken, thence the Atlantic, France, and the Great War.

The Colonel was forty-six and a graduate of United States Military Academy at West Point, Class of 1894. He was a career United States Regular Army infantryman. As a young officer, he had led troops in the Spanish-American War in Cuba and in the Philippine-American War on those Asian islands. More recently, he had trained troops in several Army camps. On March 18, 1918, he had been assigned to command the 61st Infantry Regiment, and in doing so, he took this train ride north.

Shortly before his departure from Camp Greene, his wife, Ida, and their three sons, Richard, age 10, Hugh, Jr., age 6, and John, age 4, left for New York City where they were to live until the Colonel, they hoped, would return from Europe. Before leaving, Hugh, Jr. had given his father a little lead soldier to accompany him, as a scribe. Those soldiers, he of flesh and he of lead, would experience the blood of war in the Vosges Mountains, St. Mihiel, and Meuse-Argonne.

Until he was selected to go to Europe, the life of the Little Lead Soldier had been typical of the lives of similar toy soldiers. Probably around 1900, he was created in Dresden, Germany, in the molds of the Heyde Toy Soldier Company. There he acquired the distinctive uniform of a British Dragoon, mounted infantrymen who sported scarlet tunics. His plume, however, was yellow rather than the usual white, either because he was a leader or perhaps because of artistic preference. The Colonel, who did not like things Germanic, either did not know of his companion's origin, or was able to ignore it.

Before leaving Germany, the Little Lead Soldier was placed in a box of similar soldiers and crossed the Atlantic Ocean by ship where he languished on the shelves of a New York department store until he and the others in his box were selected by the Wise family to join other soldiers in their collection. At the hands of the Wise boys, he engaged in mock battles, but nothing prepared him for what lay ahead in Europe. In the real war, he escaped artillery, bombs, shrapnel, and poisonous gas. When he returned at last from Europe, he was scratched and his head had become loose from his torso. He had lost the peg which held him to his horse and the reins to guide the horse. As for his horse, it suffered two broken legs which had to be repaired. Nonetheless, the Lead Soldier and his horse survived.

On April 5, 1918, in his first letter to Hugh, Jr., the Little Lead Soldier wrote:

Dear Hugh,

Certainly, I never expected to go to a real war and your hand must have been the hand of fate when you took me from the box and gave me to the Colonel, saying: "Here, Daddy, take this little soldier with you to write what is happening."

You remember how he laughed and replied; "Well, Hukins, he will probably know as much about it as some of us live ones."

Now, there is a lot of truth in that for many live soldiers do go to war without really knowing what it is all about nor exactly what they are fighting for.

By chance, the selective draft plucked them from their homes just as by chance your fingers selected me from among my comrades in our box. Chance has given us the good fortune of going and we must trust chance for the good fortune of returning.

But whether a man returns from this war or whether he is buried on the battlefield in France, he is fortunate in being permitted to go and do his bit for his god and his country and this fight for civilization and Christianity.

Those of us who know nothing of war will learn something of it and those who know something of it will learn more before it is over.

Being just a little lead soldier, I shall have to sit around in the Colonel's tent and travel in his dispatch case and observe like:

A wise old owl lived in an oak.
The more he saw, the less he spoke.
The less he spoke, the more he heard.
Oh, Soldier imitate that bird.

The difficulty is going to be in how to tell you what I see and hear for it is not permitted to write letters about troop movements and operations until after a time when information might be of value to the enemy. So, many of my letters will reach you long after the events they describe and some of them will not reach you until after the war.

I am not going to try to write you a history of the war but will write just what our regiment is seeing, doing, and thinking.

My! But that order to move came suddenly! Only day before yesterday you were playing around our camp and tonight you are gone with mother and the other boys on your way to New York!

I felt very sorry for the Colonel when the train left. On the way back to camp we passed the house you had just left.

Of course, he had known all along that our stay here would be only temporary and, as a matter of fact, he could not live there with us but it was a place where he could ride into from camp and see his family and when he saw that house tonight with its closed doors and dark windows, he must have realized that even that make-shift was gone and there would be no home for him till after the war.

When we reached the camp, the Adjutant reported that the train bearing the regiment's heavy impedimenta had pulled out and that all was in readiness for the entrainment of the troops in the morning. So, before you reach New York, we shall be following you.

The Embarkation Camp is near New York and I shall see you there.

It is late—the camp is all quiet—everyone but the Colonel and me is asleep—resting for tomorrow's hustle when we make our start for war.

Good night,
Your Soldier

The next day, April 6, the Lead Soldier wrote:

Dear Hugh,

Our fun at Camp Greene is over. The camp is here and other troops will be in it but our regiment will soon be gone and its camp where you used to play will be deserted.

The tents are down and along the roads there were company streets and lines of stacked rifles and, behind them, rows of piled equipment in packs which the men will throw on when the signal comes: "Fall in."

The Colonel with his field officers and staff are standing where headquarters used to be but the colors only are there to show where it is now and soon they will lead us off to the train—to the ship—to France.

The men, awaiting the assembly, are grouped about the stacks, joking and laughing or discussing what may be ahead of them.

I wonder what may be ahead of them—nothing that can daunt these men—that is certain—but serious work, I should say, for the news from the battle-front continues bad.

The fierce German offensive pushes on. They are close to Paris again and they are shelling it with big guns.

The Allies have thrown in all their strength to stem the German flood but that cannot sweep it back. They need more weight and they must have it quick. Our allies are worn by the long heroic struggle they have had and they are depleted by their awful losses of the past four years.

America can spend no more time in preparing to help them. She must throw in her millions of eager, strong, young men and she must do it now. The fight is in the balance and we must turn the scale.

They are crying for our help over there and they are no more eager for it than we are to give it. The bad news from the front makes these men only the more eager to be there—they are keen for it.

I have caught the spirit myself and I want to start. But it does make me a little sad to leave here where we've had so much fun.

You will not come out to guard mounting and parade anymore, Hukins. You cannot have Corporal Conde perch you on the Colonel's horse and lead you around the drill-field—they are both gone.

The "B" Company cooks who used to save things for you are setting their stove up in the kitchen car. The Colonel's tent is down. The cot on which you slept is rolled up with the folding chair that Mother used and they have gone to the train with the baggage. The Colonel's saddle is in its box on which Reilley [probably an orderly, whose name the Soldier spells differently at times] used to serve those fine camp breakfasts with hotcakes and molasses. The wobbly table and the smoky stove have gone to the Q.M. dump. All our familiar things have just disappeared and, in a few minutes, Camp Greene will be for us only a memory.

Those were happy days you boys had at Camp Greene and you will remember them all your lives and the Colonel will think of them many times in the trenches "over there."

The Colonel has given the signal—the battalions are forming, we are off!

So long,

Your Soldier

Entrainment from Camp Greene had gone smoothly and quietly, but it was a large undertaking and secrecy, however silly, was honored. The troop train was long and obvious. As it passed through towns, people cheered and rang bells. Sirens sounded their best wishes. At stops, Red Cross ladies boarded with sandwiches, cigarettes, and good cheer. The men were under orders not to discuss where they had been, nor where they were going. Even a casual spy, however, would know that they were headed to France.

The train ride gave the Colonel time to reflect. He had known for a long time that the German militarists had to be stopped. At the beginning of the war in 1914, they had "raped," or so it would seem, the neutral country of Belgium, massacring women and children, infuriating the civilized world. The British propagandists had concocted the Bryce Commission Report detailing German atrocities committed in Belgium, many of which were later found to be of dubious veracity. The report was available to anybody for a penny and provided tinder to inflame the American press.[1]

Many Americans clamored for war against the transgressors. Approximately 25,000 U.S. citizens crossed the ocean and joined the ranks of the Allies. Many of those volunteers were sons of the American elite and had attended acclaimed schools and universities. They were drawn to the glory of the fight for noble causes against ignoble brutish German militarists. A group of such adventurers formed the famed Lafayette Escadrille, daring aviators who engaged the Germans in what was close to hand-to-hand combat while high in the skies. The exploits of the volunteers were reported widely and skillfully by soon-to-be famous writers such as Ernest Hemingway and John Dos Passos, who were serving as volunteer ambulance drivers.

Among the most vociferous proponents of American intervention and the attendant glory of battle was former president Theodore Roosevelt, a political rival of the sitting president, Woodrow Wilson. The Rough Rider, who was almost fifty-nine years old, had contracted fevers in the Amazon basin and had a bullet near his lung from an assassination attempt in 1912.[2] Nonetheless, he sought to form a volunteer division under his command to engage the Germans as soon as possible.

Potential recruits had flocked to Roosevelt's banner, including Hugh Wise, who had met the rambunctious man in 1898 on the hills of battle in Cuba, during the Spanish-American War. Roosevelt thought highly of Wise. Beginning in 1915, the career soldier had communicated with Roosevelt requesting, and being assured of, a position of command if TR were permitted to form a division. In writing to then Major Wise, the former president exclaimed, "But, Oh Lord, there are moments when I think we are beginning to run neck and neck with the Chinese, as the greatest of the yellow nations!"

A division such as Roosevelt sought to form would number up to 20,000 troops and consist of three brigades, made up of three regiments, which, in turn, consisted of three battalions and then down the line to smaller groupings, such as companies. The larger the number of troops, the higher would be the rank of its commanding officer. Thus, subject to circumstances, generals led divisions and brigades; colonels led regiments (up to 5,000 men); majors led battalions, and so on.

In 1917, hopes of the soon-to-be-promoted Colonel (by that time he had already been promoted from Captain to Major, which Roosevelt had been told, but forgotten) were raised. He received at Schofield Barracks in Honolulu a letter from the former president and Rough Rider dated February 7:

My dear Captain Wise:

It now looks as if it were possible that I will be permitted to raise a division to serve against the Germans. If so, and if the War Department gives me a free hand, I desire to offer you a commission as Colonel of one of the regiments. If you are able to accept, I should, at the earliest possible opportunity, wish to consult with you to acquaint you with the civilians I desire to place under you in the position of Lieutenant Colonel and Majors; and to talk with you, as to the Captains we shall get.

Very Sincerely,

Theodore Roosevelt

Roosevelt's warriors would be enlisted volunteers, like the Rough Riders had been, not draftees. At that time, the merits of the opposing philosophies advanced for a volunteer army or a conscripted army were fiercely debated.[3] The Civil War riots related to conscription, although not within memory of most, were also not ancient history. There were other social issues. Southerners feared that conscription would force intermingling of races. Advocates argued that conscription would forge a national unity that would extinguish the hyphens between (whatever, such as German- or Irish-) American and foster a national identity that appeared threatened by recent immigration.

After declaring war on April 6, 1917, Congress passed the Conscription Act on May 18, but as a congressional compromise, the president was given discretion to activate up to four divisions of volunteers, to be sent forthwith to France. Immediately, by press announcement, he declined to do so, in part blaming Roosevelt for playing politics. In his May 21 letter to those who had volunteered, including the Colonel, the reciprocating Roosevelt excoriated the president for playing politics.

A disgruntled Roosevelt stated, "All four divisions would have sailed and two would have been on the firing line by September 1, the time at which the Secretary of War has announced that the assembling of the selective draft army is to begin."[4] There were to be no Roosevelt divisions. So the Colonel waited, training troops at Fort Zachary Taylor, Kentucky, until he took command of the 61st Infantry Regiment at Camp Greene, North Carolina.

On his trip north, chugging through his natal Virginia, the Colonel probably mused that the state had been the land of his ancestors for many generations. As later letters show, he wanted to emulate his father and grandfather. Henry Alexander Wise, his grandfather, had been governor of the state just before the Civil War and had been appointed a brigadier general by Confederate president Jefferson Davis. He was charged with leading an expeditionary force to preserve the Kanawha Valley in western Virginia for the Confederacy.[5] His father, John Sergeant Wise, had been one of the Virginia Military Institute cadets who attacked the Union forces at the Battle of New Market in 1864.[6] Now, here was he, Hugh Douglas Wise, their grandson and son, a colonel in the United States Army.

In reality, he never could mimic his grandfather, at whose desk he had played as a child. The governor was ambitious, egotistical and, to many, eccentric. He fomented controversies, not the least of which was when, as governor, he ordered the execution of John Brown, a fanatic who, in 1859, wanted to start a slave uprising by attacking the U.S. Army arsenal at Harpers Ferry in western Virginia. The attempt was suppressed and Brown was captured. Before ordering him executed Governor Wise met with Brown several times and professed to greatly admire him, as a man of unwavering conviction. Nonetheless, Governor Wise ordered him hanged.

The slaveholding governor, despite leading troops against the Union, never considered himself at war with the United States. He maintained that he fought as a soldier in the Army of Virginia, under the Stars and Stripes, never as a Confederate, whose buttons he never wore. Maintaining that he was not a traitor, he never sought a pardon after the war.

The Colonel's father, John Sergeant Wise, at age sixteen, was wounded in the Battle of New Market. He wrote, "Then I found I was bleeding from a long and ugly gash in the head. That rifled shell, bursting in our faces, had brought down five of us. 'Hurrah!' I thought, 'youth's dream is realized at last. I've got a wound, and am not dead yet.'"[7] He recovered and received a commission as lieutenant in the Provincial Army of the Confederate States. He also served as a captain in the Richmond Light Infantry Blues.

As his father before him had done, John represented Virginia in the U.S. House of Representatives, although, in his case, after the Civil War. He later moved with his family, including Hugh, to New York City, where he practiced law. Not much wealth accompanied them.

Both father and grandfather were "men of honor" and ticklish to perceived insult. Facing death or injury, each was a duelist. Each was a lawyer, a noted orator, and also an author.[8] On the train, the Colonel realized that he was approaching an arena in which he could stamp his own mark, hopefully, as firmly as his father and grandfather had done: the battlefield in the greatest war ever fought.

The Colonel was proud of his own achievements, but he had not yet had the type of opportunities to shine as his father and grandfather had been provided. He had begun his military training at Virginia Military Institute and then received an appointment to West Point from which he graduated in 1894. After graduating, he had been assigned to duty at Madison Barracks in Watertown, New York. He became a bicycle enthusiast and was the first bicyclist to deliver messages between military barracks to demonstrate the usefulness of that form of transportation for military purposes, in the pre-motorized era. In 1897, he established a time record for riding a bicycle from Washington,

D.C., to New York City. He also became a pioneer in flying kites with attached cameras for surveillance, the first drones.

His first combat experience had been in 1898 in Cuba during the Spanish-American War. He wrote extensive notes about his experiences. He served on the front lines and trenches with the units that he commanded. In the spring of 1899, as with many other soldiers, he contracted yellow fever. He became seriously ill and was hospitalized for five days and confined to quarters for another five days. The army surgeon reported that he was unfit for further service in the tropics, which included the Philippines, where his infantry regiment was next assigned.

Unwilling to accept restrictions, Wise, who was then a first lieutenant, went over the head of the surgeon and received permission to join his regiment in the Philippines. He spent most of the next several years, first fighting the rebels seeking independence from the United States, and later leading "Philippine scouts," fighting insurrectionists. The fighting that he described in his lengthy notes of the conflict seems similar to the later conflict in Vietnam where small bands of locals would attack and then disappear, absorbed either into the forests or blended back into their villages where they were indistinguishable from noncombatants.

Working his way up the ladder of military rank after service in the Philippines, the Colonel had graduated from the the Army School of the Line and the Army Staff College, from which he had been "Recommended to be Chief of Staff of a Division or to Command a Brigade." Climbing up, he had instructed state militias in New York, New Jersey, Pennsylvania, Kentucky, and Connecticut before being assigned to command a battalion in Hawaii. Then he became commandant of the Infantry School of Arms, Camp Zachary Taylor, and thence Camp Greene. The Colonel wanted to command a brigade as a brigadier general.

He was an athletic man of imagination and action, "a game cock" in the words of Theodore Roosevelt. Bicycling was not his only sporting activity. He loved to hunt. He had jumped his horse in the Madison Square Garden Horse Show and was pictured doing so on the cover of the November 19, 1903, issue of the popular *Leslie's Weekly Magazine*. His imagination extended beyond kite experiments with cameras; he was also a pioneer in manned kite flying and, while in the Philippines, had invented a type of bayonet adapted for the unique conditions of that terrain.[9]

Most of all, Wise was energetic. While back at Madison Barracks in Watertown, New York, on leave from duty in Cuba, the *Watertown Times* on October 7, 1898, had written, "He is probably the smallest man in the regiment, but he is made up of muscle and nerve, and fatigue and danger are words that are not in his dictionary. If an officer had a regiment of men like him they could charge the outposts of Hades and make Mephisto hang out the white flag."

But he had a secret: a bum leg.

TWO

THE DEADLY SEAS

T HE REGIMENT ARRIVED AT CAMP MERRITT, NEW JERSEY, the night of April 8, 1918, and for the next five days they waited. For the Colonel, this was far better than the six weeks, from mid-April to June 10, 1898, that he had waited in Tampa, Florida, before embarking to Cuba. In his notes at the time, he described Tampa as "a desert of hot burning dust and sand." From Camp Merritt, a far more hospitable site, the Colonel was able to visit with his family in New York City and Ida and the boys visited the camp.

Ida Hungerford Wise was the only child of Richard S. Hungerford and Adele Babcock. Both families had been prominent in upstate New York politics and financial circles. Ida was brought up in Watertown, New York, where she had met officer Hugh D. Wise when he was stationed at nearby Madison Barracks. They married in 1906, and she and her husband began their family and the peripatetic lives of a career military family.

Ida's mother and Hugh's father had died before the soldier left for France in 1918. Hugh's mother, the former Eva Douglas of Nashville, Tennessee, was close to blindness and scarcely able to care for herself. Ida's father was plagued by recurrent illness.

Hugh's departure for the war thrust upon Ida the harsh reality that she did not have a home. Apparently, that was not a concern for the United States Army in 1918. In these trying times, Ida was greatly helped by Hugh's brother Henry, his wife, Henrietta, and their family, who hosted her at their house for a while. She did not regard their generosity as a solution.

After the five-day respite, on April 14, the Colonel boarded the troop transport U.S.S. *Pocahontas*. He did not know what to expect. In going to Cuba from Tampa, he had spent fifteen days aboard a troop transport, the *Santiago*, mostly just floating around in excruciating heat, waiting for orders to disembark. He had traveled back and forth from the Philippines twice, once on a decrepit, leaky, rat-infested former coastal steamer, the *Morgan City,* which had previously been docked as "unseaworthy" and sank shortly afterward. Now, as the troops were on a much better transport, the Lead Soldier wrote:

April 14
Dear Hugh

Yesterday, when the Colonel went in to kiss you goodnight, you boys did not know that it was his last evening with you for a long, long time.

This morning, when he took you all with him to Camp Merritt, you did not know that you were seeing us start for France.

Everything is so secret that he could not talk about it even to his boys but yesterday all arrangements had been made for commencing the embarkation of our regiment today.

While Reilly was giving you breakfast this morning, the Colonel slipped out and saw the advanced detachment start for the port. When he came back, you remember, he simply smiled and said: "Goodbye boys." Mother caught her breath and said "Bon Voyage"—and she smiled too.

I tell you Hukins neither of them felt like smiling for they both knew what a heartbreaking separation was ahead of them.

Mother trembled at the dangers the Colonel was going to face. She saw him under shell-fire and in gas. He saw her anguish for the days and nights of uncertainty and pictured her breathlessly reading the casualty reports.

You boys looked on, wide-eyed, but you did not realize what an awful moment that was for them and you did not understand that they were smiling because they wanted to cry.

They knew what they were doing and they wanted to do it though it hurt cruelly. So they concealed their pain and smiled encouragement to each other.

In afterlife, remember that parting, Hukins. When an ordeal is before you, face it with a smile. A smile may not lessen the hurt but it will help you bear the pain.

When the Colonel picked up each of you boys, and hugged you, he did not speak a word. Then he took Mother in his arms but neither spoke—they could not speak but, you remember, both smiled.

Then he bounced into the automobile and whirred off, waving his hand to you and still smiling while you all shouted: "Goodbye Daddy."

That last picture of Mother and you boys, smiling him on to do his duty, is fixed in the Colonel's memory. It is a happy picture and it will cheer him up many times during the hard days to come.

But I noticed when we arrived at the railhead, where the troops were waiting to entrain, that he had to wipe his eyes before showing himself to them.

Soon we were aboard, all curtains drawn to conceal the troops and the train started for the port of embarkation. There we detrained and marched quietly onto the piers.

A high fence surrounded the piers, hiding all inside. A broad gate swung open for us—we marched in—the gates closed—we were separated from home for not even the Colonel can go out nor send a message out—we might as well be at sea. Our princess is "The Pocahantas." She was formerly the Prinzessin

Irene of the North German Lloyd Line. At the beginning of the war she sought refuge in our harbors from the British Navy. When we declared war we took her, as we did all of the German ships in our ports and changed her name.

But, in the meantime, the German crews had worked a trick on us. When they saw that our entrance into the war was probably inevitable, they tried to render the ships unseaworthy. They threw overboard important parts of the machinery, broke steam connections, cracked cylinder heads, and built fires under empty boilers.

So, when we took over the ships, none of them were fit for service. The work of our boilermakers and machinists in repairing these ships in an incredibly short time is one of the most striking instances of American efficiency in war work.

The result is that we now have a number of fine big German ships carrying us over to help whip the sneaky rascals.

* * *

The Colonel is out on deck, leaning on the rail, gazing at the lights of New York. I'll bet he is thinking of Mother and you boys and you are probably thinking or dreaming of him.

Good night,
Your Soldier

The Colonel was in charge of the 61st Infantry Regiment of the 5th Division of the United States Army, under the command of General John McMahon. It was a "regular" division, meaning that its soldiers were not part of the National Guard unit of a state. When war was declared, President Wilson had mobilized the various National Guard units into the United States Army, but they retained their separate identities, several achieving hard-earned glory. The 61st Infantry, however, consisted of career United States Army soldiers, such as the Colonel, and drafted conscripts.

The 5th Division was not the first to cross the Atlantic. That honor went to the 1st Division, which had been sent in June

1917 at the request of the French to show that demoralized country—exhausted from fighting for the previous three years—that American troops would be coming to help. Because the 1st Division was untrained in the trench warfare that dominated the arena, its initial mission was symbolic.

For more than a century before the war, the British had dominated the seas: "Rule, Britannia, rule the waves." In the 1890s, however, Germany began to build a competing navy. By the time the conflict began, its navy was still inferior to that of the British, but only the Germans had submarines, called U-boats. The German surface fleet spent the early years of the war bottled up in the North Sea by the British fleet that barred its exit from that limited area. In the only major naval battle of the war, at Jutland on May 31–June 1, 1916, Germany probably won by the number of ships sunk and sailors killed, but its fleet was badly damaged. It gave up large-scale encounters and remained at anchor at Wilhelmshaven and Kiel for the duration of the war, until scuttled by German mutineers near the end of the war.

With the German surface fleet on the sidelines, the Atlantic would have been a closed British lake were it not for the U-boats. They were not confined in the North Sea, and by the end of the war, the U-boats had sunk 5,282 merchant ships.[1] The submarine was a sneaky, cowardly beast. Out of sight, it could slink undetected until close to its prey and then launch its torpedoes for the kill.

On May 7, 1915, off the coast of Ireland, the submarine U-20 sank the grand British passenger liner *Lusitania,* on its way from New York to London, killing over 1,000 civilians, of whom 123 were Americans. Even though the German embassy had published newspaper warnings that Americans, citizens of a self-declared neutral country, were at risk in traveling to Europe on ships flying the British flag, Americans were outraged. An indignant President Wilson scolded and lectured the Germans on the principles of humanity. Fearing that loss of American lives would cause the United States to declare war against them, the Germans relented in September 1915 and promised not to sink passenger liners without warning. Such warnings would at least permit some passengers to board lifeboats.

Maritime trade with America provided the essentials for Britain to wage war, and even to survive. In exchange, the trade provided enormous profits to American businesses which were manufacturing and shipping to the British. Financed by credits from American banks, in the early months of 1917, the British were spending the equivalent of $75 million weekly for American goods and munitions.[2] Americans demanded "Freedom of the Seas," which really meant, "Germans, do not interfere with our trade with Britain."

A British blockade of German ports meant that the British Royal Navy would search American vessels and those of other countries for "contraband" and confiscate it, if found. The blockade effectively cut off American trade with Germany. Trade from other neutral countries was severely limited.[3] Food and fertilizer were scarce. The winter of 1916 was particularly hard. Many German civilians starved. The country was desperate.

In the winter of 1916 a debate raged in Germany. There were those who wanted to pursue peace, but the navy was convinced that the war could be won by "unrestricted" submarine warfare. In 1915 there had only been 54 U-boats. In 1916 another 108 had been built.[4] Unrestricted submarine warfare meant that the submarines would no longer give warnings and would attack all shipping coming into the British Isles, regardless of the flag being flown. Inevitably, American ships would be sunk and, almost inevitably, the United States would declare war on Germany in vindication of the principle of freedom of the seas for neutral nations.

The German high command figured that it would take five months of unrelenting submarine attacks on merchant shipping to starve the British Isles. They calculated that the unprepared Americans would not be able to deploy a significant force in that short period of time and that the British would seek peace, acceding to German demands.

The Germans were right that the Americans were almost totally unprepared. After the Civil War, there had been no need for massive mobilization. Ridding the Americas of the Spanish in the Spanish-American War in 1898 and the Philippine adventure in the early years of the 1900s had not required much manpower or weaponry. The same was true of the unrest on the Mexican border which ended in February 1917 after a futile American chase in Mexico of the warlord "bandit" Pancho Villa, whose men had crossed the border and murdered sixteen Americans at Columbus, New Mexico.

The Mexican foray had only involved 15,000 men, with some National Guard units in the rear, protecting the border.[5] In early 1917 there were only 100,000 regular Army soldiers.[6] The Americans ranked seventeenth in the world in number of professional soldiers.[7] Meager pay and infrequent promotion for the regular Army men resulted in much voluntary attrition of the ranks.[8] Including conscripts, the World War I Army of the United States grew to 4 million men by the time of the armistice eighteen months later.[9]

Although he had ordered the chase of Pancho Villa, which had the stated purpose of protecting the border and an incidental goal of protecting American oil and railroad business interests, President Wilson thought of himself as a pacifist and idealist. Coming from a family of Presbyterian ministers, he also wore the stripes of an evangelical moralist.

Before the United States declared war, Wilson thought of himself as a messiah on a mission to save European peoples from themselves. He ardently wanted to broker a peace that would end the conflict. He entreated the warring leaders to use his good services to mediate. When that did not work, he called for the people of the world to seek peace, even if their governments would not do so.

The stubborn and unenlightened Europeans, however, were intransigent in pushing for victory. For them, peace without victory, as proposed by Wilson, was not acceptable. Each side felt that its people had lost too much to leave the battle without something to show for the enormous sacrifices that had been made.

Wilson's efforts were repeatedly rebuffed, but he continued to try. Historian Barbara Tuchman comments:

> The facts [the intransigence of the combatants] would have forced themselves upon anyone but Wilson, but the armor of fixed purpose he wore was impenetrable. He chose two main principles—neutrality for America, negotiated peace for Europe—as the fixed points of his policy and would allow no realities to interfere with them. . . . Although no two men in any one period of history were more unlike, Wilson shared one characteristic with the Kaiser—he would not listen to opinions he did not welcome. Wilhelm was afraid of them, but Wilson considered opinions which opposed his as simply a waste of time. Intent upon saving Europe, he ignored the mood of the Europeans.[10]

On December 18, 1916, Wilson had asked the warring governments to state their war aims. By January 12, 1917, both sides had rejected that overture. Unknown to the president, on January 10, Kaiser Wilhelm had signed an order for unrestricted submarine warfare, aiming to starve the British before the Americans could effectively mobilize.

On January 31, the German ambassador to the United States delivered to the American secretary of state a note saying that on the next day unrestricted submarine warfare would resume. The president decided to sever diplomatic relations with Germany, but that step did not cause the Germans to retract their declaration.

While the U.S. Congress was jousting about whether to arm merchant ships to try to deter U-boat attacks, the British gave President Wilson a decoded telegram from German foreign minister Zimmermann to German ambassador von Bernstorff, who was stationed in Washington. The British had intercepted that telegram from a special cable that the president had authorized

Germany to use for communications between the Fatherland and its ambassador for the purpose of facilitating peace negotiations. Rather than for that purpose, Zimmermann told the German ambassador to contact German diplomats in Mexico and instruct them to invite Mexico to ally itself with Germany and attack the United States.

The bait that the Germans offered was the chance to regain the territory that Mexico had lost almost sixty years earlier in the Mexican-American War of 1848. The swath of land comprised a large part of the present-day western United States. The diplomats were also to encourage Japan to join the German effort. (Japan wanted the American-owned Panama Canal.)

When the decoded message was given to the president and he was informed that it had been sent over the special German cable and intercepted by the British, he was outraged, not only by the import of the message, but also at the Germans' effrontery in using the cable that had been authorized to facilitate peace negotiations. The pious Presbyterian president exclaimed, "Good Lord! Good Lord!"[11]

The telegram was given to the Associated Press and duly published. In oversize type, the March 1 front-page headline of the *New York Times* blared: "GERMANY SEEKS AN ALLIANCE AGAINST US; ASKS JAPAN AND MEXICO TO JOIN HER; FULL TEXT OF HER PROPOSAL MADE PUBLIC."

Then, the U-boats started sinking American ships. Three went down on March 21. Even though it meant agreeing with archcritic Theodore Roosevelt, Wilson requested a declaration of war and Congress complied on April 6, 1917. Some historical reviewers point out that British credit had just been exhausted as of April.[12] Britain no longer had credit with which to buy American goods, and if Britain lost the war, there would not be much chance of being paid back.

With full knowledge of the dangers of submarine attack, the American 1st Division, commanded by General Robert Lee Bullard and composed in part of veterans of the Mexican Campaign, embarked to cross the seas in June 1917. As described by

General Bullard, it was a lengthy voyage with constant zig-zagging, whistle alerts, and fear.[13] He was sure that his ship had been pursued and unsuccessfully attacked. He recorded, "at 12 p.m., a submarine alarm was sounded by my transport. I was out of bed before the sound ceased, finding that the ship's watch had seen coming toward us, at an angle, what was either a torpedo or a great fish, stirring up the phosphorescence. Our ship stopped, the object passed across our bow and was seen no more."[14]

The threat was more than theoretical. On February 5, 1918, the U-boats had bagged the troop ship *Tuscania*, and on May 23, 1918, *Moldovia*, another troop ship, sank after being struck by a U-boat torpedo. In April 1918, Colonel Wise was aware of the peril awaiting the trip.

For the troops on *Pocahontas*, at first, novelty prevailed. While still at dock, the Lead Soldier wrote:

U.S. Navy Transport *Pocahontas*
Point of Embarkation
15 April 18
Dear Hugh:
    Today has been a busy one. Yesterday the detachment which came aboard with us made preparations for the regiment which began arriving at 9:00 a.m. today. All was ready for them and I was surprised to see how quickly and easily all their impedimenta and equipment can be embarked when it is done with order and with system.

* * *

The men's quarters are in what used to be the second cabin and the cargo holds. These have been remodeled and arranged for light and ventilation and fresh air is forced into them through flues like big furnace flues in a house so that, in spite of the great number of men, the air is always sweet and cool.

The bunks are four high, in parallel rows, with just room to walk between them. The uprights and frames are of iron and the beds are steel springs so they are easily kept clean. The bunks can be turned up to make room and to give opportunity for inspection. There are not mattresses for they would cause dirt and consume air space. The men just put their blankets on the springs and, every fair day, they are taken up and aired on deck.

All the decks and quarters are iron so they can be flushed and easily cleaned and every hold has its wash troughs and shower baths convenient.

The cooking is done in great steam kitchens called "galleys" outside of which are the big serving tables. At mealtimes the men line up with their mess pans and cups and pass these tables where their food is served to them. Then they go off and find a place where they can sit on the deck and eat.

There is no luxury in this way of living but the men are comfortable and the food is good and abundant so they will be well and healthy when they arrive in France to face the Boche (derogatory slang for German).

The officers are quartered in the state rooms and mess in the ship's salon which is the most interesting place because it is decorated with German paintings and the Prussian Eagle looks down from the stained glass skylight. I guess that old bird feels out of place here for, certainly, he has no friends on this ship.

By noon, the regiment was embarked and baggage all loaded. . . .

THE COLONEL'S DESCRIPTION of the living conditions on the transport differs from that given by some others. Under pressure from the British and French, the Americans were trying to transport as many troops as quickly as possible across the Atlantic. That meant crowding. One description follows: "For many of them [the soldiers on a ship transport] the shipping problem meant only one thing—a grueling voyage and a sharp lesson in military indifference. The most powerful memory most of them had of the war was not the death-or-glory episodes of taking a machine-gun nest by storm, nor even the delights of French vin blanc, but of the crowded, sickening, filthy conditions in which they had traveled across the Atlantic Ocean to arrive at Brest or St. Nazaire."[15]

Historian Gary Mead quotes Lieutenant Donnelly describing his trip over on *America* sailing on February 27, 1918: "[The enlisted men] were quartered in the holds in tiers of bunks, four bunks high. At night all portholes were closed as a protection against detection from submarines, and the ventilation was poor. The smell emanating from these holds was enough to make one sick without any assistance from rough weather. . . . Things were miserable down in the troop quarters; they were bad enough during smooth sailing but now [during rough weather] to the smell of foul air and sweat was added the sickening odor of sour vomit."[16]

Those conditions were made even worse by overcrowding. A month after the Colonel sailed, an order was entered that required three men for each two berths, which increased by 50 percent the number of soldiers that could be transported on each crossing.[17] Even worse, in the summer and fall, the flu epidemic struck, aided by the awful conditions. Bodies of the flu victims were returned to America on the ships on which they had left.

For the voyage of the Colonel, the overcrowding order had not yet been given and the flu bug had not arrived. On April 16, 1918, the Lead Soldier wrote:

Onboard Transport *Pocahontas*
Port of Embarkation
16 April 18
Dear Hugh:
Right after breakfast this morning, a handsome big ship glided into the dock and made fast to the pier opposite us. She is "The Mount Vernon" and was formerly "The Prinzessen Ce-celie" of the North German Lloyd Line. Now she is an American transport.

Early in the war, she attempted to go from the United States to Germany with millions of dollars in gold for the German government. She was never to get there, for a few days later she returned to the United States pursued by British cruisers and claimed refuge at Bar Harbor. After she had stayed the 24 hours allotted her under international law she was interned and the money was placed in the U.S. sub-treasury for safekeeping. But when we declared war with Germany she became an enemy ship and we took her over, and, as money is contraband of war, we took also those millions of gold dollars.

In the meantime, however, her crew, like the crews of other German ships in our ports, tried to render her unseaworthy. We repaired the damage and there she is—one of our biggest, finest, fastest transports—just back from France where she delivered more than 5000 troops, having made the round trip in less than three weeks.

* * *

We were still watching the Mount Vernon when a sailor man ran up, saluted and said "The Captain's compliments and would the Colonel come to the Captain's room."

When the Colonel came out, he sent for his adjutant and said: "All men below decks till further orders—not a bit of cocky to show on this ship." I wondered what it was all about but very soon the ship began to tremble—glided back out of the slip—the hawsers were off—we were on our way to France.

From the table where I sat, I saw the skyscrapers of New York drop behind us. Governor's Island slipped by. We passed the Statue of Liberty standing holding the light that we were going to try to help spread over the world. Is it not splendid, Hukins, that we were going to have a part in this fight for civilization?

When we were well out beyond the narrows, restrictions were removed and the men piled up onto the decks. All around us were other ships—queer looking things—all mottled and streaked and splashed with irregular designs and different colors to "camouflage" them or make them more difficult to see and aim at.

A navy cruiser was steaming around among the fleet putting it in formation as an old duck does with her flock. As she passed us her band was playing "Where Do We Go From Here Boys?" And our band answered by playing "Over There."

* * *

There were fourteen ships in our convoy, carrying about 25,000 men, that is a lot of men but in this war it is but a handful. But the United States is throwing in these handfuls very fast and it will be soon be a France—full of American soldiers.

* * *

Our fleet is in formation now and is steaming out to sea—three ships abreast in three columns guarded by the cruisers.

New York has disappeared astern, Sandy Hook is only a line on the horizon. Our next land will be "over there."

Your Soldier

By 1918, the U-boat threat had been reduced by use of the convoy system. *Pocahontas* was a part of such a convoy. The threat, however, was far from gone. Then there was the tedium, but it was far less than that the Colonel had endured bobbing around the sweltering Caribbean waiting for the chance to land in Cuba. As he often did in down times, the Colonel put pen to paper. The Lead Soldier mitigated the boredom, but perhaps passed some of it on, by writing:

U.S.S. *Pocahontas*
At Sea
17 April 18
Dear Hugh:

It was the Navy reveille that awakened us this morning for, while on a Navy transport, we follow the Navy calls except for formations of the troops alone.

When I waked I was just conscious of a gentle swaying motion, a swish-swish sound, and a snappy salt flavor in the air, then I realized where I was.

* * *

The Huns would like nothing better than to sink one of these big transports and they are watching for us. But, believe me, we are watching for them too.

We have watches and lookouts and listening posts all around the ship and the gunners of the four guns we carry never leave their guns. The gunpointer sits right at his loaded gun ready to turn his muzzle on any periscope that pokes above the water.

Way up in the tops of the foremast and mainmast are things like huge canvas buckets. These are the "crow's nests." In each of them, two young officers are on constant watch—looking with their glasses for any sight of a U-boat, a streak of white foam, a swirl on the surface, a patch of oil, or a periscope. Looking down from up there, very small things are noticeable and nothing is too unimportant to be reported.

Our officers are not used to this crow's nest business and are not very keen for it. One has to climb up a long rope ladder and clamber over the rigging. When he gets into the crow's nest he finds it a very unsteady perch. A little movement of the ship sends the crow's nest doing merry circles and when the sea is rough it swings way out over the water first on one side and then on the other.

There are watches from the deck and watchers from the bow and watchers from the stern—all looking and listening for submarines.

Some of the watches are in enclosed places near the water level where they have a flat view and where they are cut off from the noise of the ship so that they can hear a sub. And the ship has her detector apparatus. We are defying the U boats and we even laugh at them but we are not taking any unnecessary chances with them.

Besides the submarine watches there are guards to keep order, prevent fire, and enforce sanitation.

All around the ship are tubs for trash, cigarette butts and etcetera and nothing may be thrown overboard—not even a burnt match for they might serve a sub to track the convoy.

As soon as "abandon ship drill" is over there is a gun drill. We carry 4 guns, 2 forward and 2 aft. They are manned by the sailors and about all the sailors have to do with them is to furnish the details for the ammunition hoists and shell passers. The rest of the soldiers simply keep out of the way.

* * *

From 2 o'clock till 4 is taken up with more drill and more inspections and at 5 o'clock p.m., supper.

Then the band comes on deck and plays till dark and then the men turn in for they are tired and ready to sleep.

There are no lights on the ship after dark—not even a match can be struck nor is smoking permitted for even the glow of a pipe might show a lurking submarine where to loose off a torpedo.

In the gangways and holds, there are a few very dim blue lights but none of the lights are lighted at all except the Captain's office, the chart room and the adjutant's office. These rooms are battened and the doors arranged so that the light goes out when the door is opened.

It is almost dark now so I must stop.

Good Night,

Your Soldier

Then, the apprehension. The Lead Soldier wrote:

U.S.S. *Pocahontas*
At Sea
27 April 18
Dear Hugh,

We have been in the zone for several days but about the only difference that makes is that we are all a little more on the qui-vive and everyone is required to wear the lifejacket day and night.

* * *

We now know that we are going to France for our convoy has split and the other part of it has headed north for England. We were all guessing whether we are going to Bordeaux, Brest, or Saint Nazaire but this afternoon the orders were wirelessed to us to land at Brest.

For several days the principal topic for speculation has been "When will the destroyers join us?"

Of course, the closer a convoy gets to Europe the more danger there is from U boats, so, about a day or two out, a squadron of destroyers usually joins the convoy and guards it to land.

The exact time when the destroyers will join a convoy is not known and this gave a fine opportunity for a "pool" or guessing game as to the hour and minute they would join us. Some of the younger officers got it up and the Colonel approved on condition that the winner give 10% of the pool to the band fund.

They had a merry time with it in the saloon yesterday and the man who held the ticket for 5:30 this morning won for just at that time, as daylight was spreading over the ocean, eleven smudges of smoke appeared on the horizon and very soon eleven destroyers were recognized rushing towards us. How they came! It seemed but a few minutes till they reached us.

They are beautiful graceful little ships—very low and narrow and keen and businesslike and extremely fast.

When they met us, two turned and led us, two went on each side of the convoy, two dropped behind and two went into our formation among the transports. Those outside the convoy began to do figure eights and those inside weaved in and out among the transports. It makes one think of bird dogs quartering around a field and they have kept this up all day so no submarine would dare risk being run over by them in coming too close to the transports.

All the time one of the destroyers has kept way ahead cruising about and watching.

It makes us feel very safe to have these fellows with us for there is nothing a submarine fears more than destroyers. Destroyers are so fast and quick in turning that it is hard for a sub to escape her. Then too, the destroyer is built for ramming and her sharp bow will cut through a sub as a knife cuts through a cucumber. The draft of a destroyer is so shallow that a torpedo, adjusted for depth so as to hit a big ship below the water line will pass harmlessly under the destroyer.

The destroyer is herself equipped with torpedo tubes and fairly bristles with quick firing guns. But what the sub most fears are the deadly depth bombs she carries. These are large tanks filled with high explosives. If a destroyer locates a submerged submarine, she dashes to the vicinity and lets go a depth bomb which sinks down near the submarine and explodes. The tremendous concussion cracks the thin skin of the U boat and she and her crew of pirates head for the nearest land—straight down.

With 11 destroyers protecting us, I think we can feel fairly easy in daytime but at night the destroyers cannot be so much among us and a sub might get in and loose off a torpedo.

That is why we have to be so careful about lights and even for navigation, only one light shows. That is the pencil light astern. It is a small light in a tube which points straight astern to guide the ship following.

Good Night,
Your Soldier

Despite all precautions, the convoy was spotted. The appropriate warnings and alarms were sounded, but there was no overt attack.[18] They made it. "There" had become "here," Brest, the westernmost port in France. The Lead Soldier wrote:

Pontenezin Barracks, Brest
28 April 18
Dear Hugh,

Certainly, the news before we sailed and the wireless news we have received on the way across was far from reassuring and what we are now hearing is no more so for, though the Boche drive seems to have been brought to a stop, he has held most of his gains and he seems to be either more or as much the master of the situation as he was a year ago.

We did not fool ourselves with a belief that we were coming over to immediately take part in a triumphal march into Germany but we are a little surprised to find the situation no better than it is—that it is a lot worse than you people at home realize.

There is a lot of hard campaigning and bloody fighting ahead of us before Fritz (slang for Germans) goes back across the Rhine but he has got to go and we are all perfectly confident of final, complete victory.

Just as we entered the harbor of Brest this morning, the clouds which were casting gloom over everything lifted and the glorious golden sunshine coated the country. It was like a good omen that our entry into France should be brightened as the entry of American troops into the war has brightened the hopes of Christendom.

We are not the first American troops to arrive but, as more of them, we are evidence that they are coming in a continuous or ever-increasing stream.

It should look good to these people and it does look good to them for, as our ship glided into the harbor, with the regimental colors unfurled on the bridge and our band playing, the people on shore went wild with enthusiasm.

It was noon when we were made fast and then, without a moment's delay, the work of the debarking, discharging, and coaling commenced.

Actually, troops were marching down the gangway, cargo was being hoisted out of the holds, and coal was coming in—all at the same time—the ship sails for New York tomorrow.

The regiment formed in the street outside the pier and marched off to Pontenezin Barracks, the band playing our regimental air—I, in the Colonel's dispatch case at the head of the regiment.

All along the route, the crowds in the streets cheered and waved flags and threw flowers and hailed us as heroes who had come to help save France. It was a proud day for us!

Pontenezin Barracks is a historical place just outside of Brest.

It was one of Napoleon's Casernes and it looks as though his soldiers might still be there. A high stone wall encloses the great bare courtyard with its rows of one-story slate roofed barracks.

In these barracks the troops are quartered. Several of them are reserved for officers but their only extra luxury is the springless iron cots which are not much more comfortable than the even flagstone floors on which the men sleep.

One little room is set aside as a regimental office and at night, it is the bedroom for the Colonel and his staff.

It is quite different from our royal suite on the ship but "C'est la guerre" and it probably is better than what we were going to have—but I feel as though we were living in a stable.

In this interesting old place, the years seem to have turned back and one feels that he belongs at Bonaparte's army. I half expect to see men of the old guard, in high shakos and tight white breeches, stalking about the court. The snappy American sentries, with magazine rifles look out of place by the quaint old iron gates and it does not seem at all fitting that our baggage should arrive in buzzing motor truck instead of in big carts drawn by huge white horses like we see in pictures.

Here, at Brest, is where Napoleon dreamed of establishing a naval base for the invasion of England. But, when anyone has dreams of conquering the Anglo-Saxon race, he'd better wake up and go to sleep right.

Napoleon got his awakening when he went up against the British at Waterloo and the rest of his dreaming was done at St. Helena.

What would Napoleon, at Waterloo, have given for just one regiment like ours—equipped as we are! With its 3000 high-power magazine rifles that can shoot accurately further than his artillery could throw a cannon ball. With 200 automatic rifles that pour streams of bullets. Our hand grenades and rifle grenades whose explosion is more powerful than that of his old artillery bombshell. Our 12 Stokes mortars, each of which can throw 30 shells a minute, each shell detonating with a force Napoleon never imagined. Our battery of pretty little 1-pounders (37 mm) so light that a couple of men can carry one, so small as to be able to hide in a brush pile, as accurate as a rifle and almost as quick-firing, with a range greater than Napoleon's heaviest field artillery and with a terribly destructive little high explosive shell. Our machine gun companies, each with 16 guns that alone could have swept the field at Waterloo clean. Our signal platoon with its apparatus, its telegraphs, its telephones, its wireless. Our pioneer platoon with it modern inventions—motorcycles, motorcars and trucks.

If Napoleon could have had one such regiment when the enemy did not have it, it could have made the Iron Duke look like a tin weathervane—couldn't he?

But, by the time you command a regiment, things will have so changed and so advanced that you will probably chuckle with amusement at the arms and equipment that we now consider so marvelous—just as the Colonel does at the funny old things his father's soldiers fought with.

Good Night,
Your Soldier

THREE

WHY?

FTER ARRIVING AT THE HARBOR IN BREST, THE LEAD
Soldier had begun his letter of April 28, 1918, by saying, "Certainly, the news before we sailed and the
wireless news we have received on the way across was far from
reassuring and what we are now hearing is no more so." The
German attack which had started on April 9 near Ypres, while
the Colonel was at Camp Merritt waiting to embark, had
achieved substantial success. Their goal had been to reach the
Channel coast and, although they had not yet done so, they had
captured vital high ground in Flanders and stood poised to resume their push. To the south, the Germans caught their breath
about seventy miles from Paris, perched to take that treasure.

There was little time to lose in Brest. A war had to be fought
and the barracks had to be evacuated before the next troops arrived. The 61st Infantry Regiment, commanded by Colonel
Wise, was part of the 5th Division of the American Expeditionary Force, led by General John McMahon. It needed to go
to a training ground closer to the front. The Lead Soldier wrote:

On a Troop Train
30 April 18
Dear Hugh,

Have you ever thought what a job it is to unload all the baggage and equipment of a regiment from a ship, sort it over, separate it into classes and by organizations, reload it into wagons and trucks, haul it to the train, and load it into the cars so that on arrival at the destination, the first things out will be the first things needed?

Well, that is what the regiment had to do yesterday and it required about five hundred men all day and all night.

This morning, the troops for the 1st section of the train marched down to the railway yards and entrained.

Entraining over here is not so easy for us as it was at home for the little European cars are not so convenient as our big cars and the railroads are not so well handled as are ours. So there were long waits and tedious delays before we finally got aboard.

These are funny little cars. They are like the pictures that you have seen in magazines. They have high wheels, doors on the sides and running-boards like an automobile.

The passenger cars have three or four compartments, each for twelve passengers. But on a train there are not enough passenger cars for all the soldiers, most of whom travel in freight cars. These are all marked "Hommes quarante, chevaux huit" (forty men, eight horses) to show how many horses or men may travel in them.

Altogether, the freight cars are more comfortable because it is easier to loll around on the floor than sit bolt-up-right in a crowded seat.

* * *

This country, Brittany, we are passing through is marvelously beautiful. It is more natural and less artificial than I expected to see in France and is not unlike parts of our own eastern country.

Spring is here in all its full beauty. The country is emerald— All green and all shades of green. It seems to me I never before saw such wondrous greens nor a country so lavishly covered with green. And all over this green covering are splashed patches of brilliant yellow and red or soft pink and purple.

God seems to have camouflaged this part of France to conceal the misery and sorrow of its people.

It is difficult to look at this fairyland and realize that but a few miles from here the most awful of wars is going on.

The villages and towns are as picturesque as the country is beautiful. They nestle down in the valleys, their soft grays and browns blending with the color about them and their slate roofs and quaint gables looking like toy models on a painted landscape.

Now and then we dash past an old castle that stands like a record of past centuries, as it is, and we almost expect to see about it bowmen and armored knights, for all about these castles have former wars been fought.

The people too are picturesque, the women in their high waisted dresses and white caps, the men in their short jackets, knee breeches and high sugar-loaf hats.

All the people are trying to be cheerful and to keep up the appearance of happiness, but they show the strain they have been under and the apprehension they are still under.

Everywhere are the signs of mourning but the faces that look from under mourning veils smile confidently for the victory that we have come to help win.

There are no able-bodied young men to be seen and few young women for they are all at the front or in war work. The old men, old women and children are working the farms and tending the homes and they are splendid in their faith, determination and sacrifice.

As we roll along they welcome us—The old men straighten up and salute, the old women wave their aprons and the pink-cheeked boys and girls shout "Hurrah pour les Americains."

They all greet us as heroes and seem to have implicit faith in our power to save them from the Boche.

* * *

It is getting dark now. The sun has gone down in a blaze of glory. Tomorrow's light will find us closer to the front where the fate of civilization is being decided.

Goodnight,

Your Soldier

As he rode through the beautiful French countryside, Colonel Wise probably thought of what brought him and the men under his command to be fighting a war in Europe, a continent from which his forebearers and those of so many other Americans had left, often fleeing from the ravages of war and what followed. Most Americans, including the Colonel, who had British and Scottish ancestors, traced their heritage to that continent. A large number had even come from Germany. The Census of 1910 showed 1,337,000 Americans had been born in Germany and an estimated 10 million were of German descent.[1] In that same census, it was reported that one of every three Americans had been born abroad or had at least one parent who had been born abroad. A total of 12 million immigrants had arrived on American shores since the turn of the century.[2]

It seemed as if one European war or another had been going on forever and allegiances were haphazard. The Seven Years' War of 1756–1763 had aligned now-enemies Britain and Prussia, the most powerful of the Germanic states, together against now-enemies France and Austria. America owed its independence to a war between now-allies France and Britain. The Napoleonic Wars of 1799–1815 pitted the French aggressors against their World War I allies, the British, who led a variety of coalitions that, at times, included their World War I enemies, Prussia and Austria. The Crimean War of 1854 pitted France and England against their World War I ally, Russia.

In 1917, most countries were governed by hereditary monarchies and privileged landowners who were now becoming industrialists. The royalty and aristocracy intermarried, as they had been doing for several centuries. They were family, or, at least, a club with selective admittance. Britain's King George V was a cousin to both Kaiser Wilhelm II of Germany and Tsar Nicholas II of Russia. In correspondence in English, the kaiser and tsar addressed each other as "Willy" and "Nicky."[3] The kaiser even held an honorary commission in the British navy. Like many families, they had their squabbles, but unlike others, they could order stand-ins to fight to the death to resolve their differences.

Leading to this particular European war, World War I, was competition between the usual suspects. The Franco-Prussian War of 1870–1871 had been quickly resolved by a Prussian victory, as a result of which Prussia (Germany) had taken the valuable border area Alsace-Lorraine from France. Germany was greedy. The kaiser wanted more territory, more colonies, more trade, and more money. That meant that Germany needed more ships, arms, and railroads and began acquiring them. For self-protection, to further their own self-interest, and to keep up, France, Britain, and Russia did the same.

The June 28, 1914, assassination of Archduke Franz Ferdinand of Austria was the nominal event that led to the war. The assassin was a Serbian nationalist. That killing provoked the dual monarchy of Austria-Hungary, with the encouragement or acquiescence of Germany, to make demands on Serbia, that, as an independent nation, it would not accept. Austria-Hungary, Serbia, and Russia had been competing for territory and influence in the always troublesome Balkans. Russia, which coveted a warm-water port leading to the Mediterranean Sea, sided with Serbia, whose residents were fellow Slavs and followers of the Orthodox Catholic religion.

Quickly, there were mobilizations of Austria-Hungary, Serbia, Russia, Germany, and France, each of which was scared of what the mobilization of each potential enemy might mean for it. On August 1, 1914, Germany declared war on Russia, on August 3 on France, and on August 4 it invaded neutral Belgium. That night, Britain, which did not want Belgium replaced by Germany directly across the English Channel from it, declared war on Germany.

Certainly, the Colonel knew that he and his men were not riding the train in France to vindicate the assassination of Franz Ferdinand. Other events, yet to occur, could have led to the same declarations of war. The conflict spread quickly over the globe, to the Near and Far East and Africa, becoming a "world war," the first of its kind. It was so horrific that many thought that it could never be allowed to happen again. Hence, it came to be commonly called "the war to end all wars."

There were many who questioned "why?" Why were the Europeans killing one another again? Why were the Americans dragged into it? Why leave family and cross the ocean to kill and be killed? Where in the world were the Balkans, anyway?

For almost all Americans there was reason, or at least rationalization. Espousing neutrality, while American businesses reaped enormous economic profit, President Wilson had tried his very best to keep American soldiers out of the European conflict. He was a liberal Democrat, bent upon a domestic economic program to curb the excesses of scarcely regulated capitalism. Conglomerate trusts, exercising almost monopolistic powers over workers and the public, were often in violent confrontation with workers who had joined together to form labor unions. Their conflicts brought mayhem and death to Americans. Why seek the same elsewhere?

President Wilson wanted his focus, for the good of the country, on solving the labor strife and addressing internal economic disparity. He presented a "New Freedom" agenda. His 1916 re-election campaign had been built on the slogan, "He kept us out of war." Wilson won in a close election which could have been lost by a change of 4,000 votes in California. Involvement in the European war would derail his domestic agenda.

Labor unrest was a problem in many capitalist countries. Across national boundaries, working-class men and women were beginning to question whether their affinity should be to their fellow workers in other countries rather than to their fellow countrymen, a group that included the capitalists who were unfairly pocketing the profits produced by their labor. In the United States, there was a strong socialist movement led by Eugene V. Debs, who had garnered 900,000 votes in the 1912 presidential election. The European socialist movement had been gaining strength even before war was declared. When war was looming, European socialists met in July 1914 in Brussels and passed an antiwar resolution. In that same month, there was an antiwar demonstration of 100,000 in Germany. Socialists were questioning why they should kill each other.

From the beginning of the war, there had been a strong British peace movement that was closely linked to the women's vote campaign. In 1916, because of the enormous death tolls, Britain instituted conscription, but provided exemptions for conscientious objectors (COs) and the Irish, who were trying to free themselves from British control. Conscription led to antiwar demonstrations and petitions for a negotiated peace. People were questioning "why?" Before the end of the war, more than 20,000 conscripts had refused to enter the British forces. Declining alternative service, more than 6,000 went to jail.[4] Having been denied CO status, some were sent to the front, where they refused to fight and were sentenced to death.

Eminent British philosopher Bertrand Russell campaigned long and hard against the war, eventually ending up behind bars. Historian Adam Hochschild summarizes Russell's opposition as follows: "He hated German militarism, he always said, loved the tradition of English liberty, and would prefer an Allied victory to a German one. But the longer the war went on, the more it was militarizing Britain in Germany's image, while killing and maiming men by the millions and making certain an embittered and dangerous postwar world."[5]

In April 1917, French troops had embarked on an ambitious offensive at Chemin des Dames. After five days and enormous losses the attack was abandoned. Immediately after, the "Mutinies of 1917" began. French troops refused to march into the slaughter but would hold defensive positions. They would reason and question "why?" They would not march into the jaws of the enemy to die senselessly. Both the troops and the populace were demoralized. For the French, war had lost its glamour.

According to author-historian John Dos Passos, who served as a volunteer ambulance driver before the United States entered the war, "Once Woodrow Wilson had formed an opinion it became to his mind the cause of righteousness. If you were to disagree you were either a knave or a fool."[6] There were some knaves and fools in the United States, and contrary to his expressed liberal principles, the president would have none of it. He took steps leading to the militarization of American democracy, just as Bertrand Russell feared was occurring in Britain. On June 15, 1917, Wilson signed into law the Espionage Act, which he had first proposed three months earlier, and eleven months later the Sedition Act, which amended the 1917 act. The legislation came close to violating the guarantee of free speech embodied in the First Amendment of the Constitution. The legislation ensnared socialist leader Debs, among others.

In an attempt to limit the knavery and foolery, the president authorized a massive propaganda effort led by newspaperman George Creel and a group of appointees who bore the title "Committee on Public Information." Successfully propagandized and without the baggage of past losses in the preceding three years, almost all Americans answered the call to arms, although there were more than 500 draftees who refused both military and alternative service.[7]

Reason gave way to virulent nationalism, enforced by occasional vigilantism. German-born Robert Prager was hanged in Missouri.[8] Bound, gagged, and stripped to the waist, pacifist clergyman Herbert S. Bigelow had his back brutally lashed to ribbons by a white-robed man with a blacksnake whip. In the cause of nationalism, Americans could inflict atrocities upon their own people.

Hate trumps reason. Hate motivates troops. According to General Bullard, one of the foremost American generals, hate started at the commander-in-chief. "More powerful and of wider reach as a hate-maker was the impression produced by the President's far-published idea that the war was nothing else than a life-and-death struggle of democracy on the side of the Allies, against autocracy on the side of the Germans."[9] Given the origins of the war, Bullard did not agree. Nonetheless, he published all instances of German cruelty and atrocities to inspire hatred of the enemy.[10]

Colonel Wise, a thoughtful man, probably questioned "why?" But he had an answer and no qualms about it: He was fighting for civilization and Christianity. Nonetheless, had his role been different, he might have questioned why his enemy professed the same Christianity and concern for civilization. He might have questioned why he and the men that he would command to victory, dismemberment, and death had to come from afar to settle one of the never-ending European disputes.

If the Colonel's wife, Ida, ever questioned "why?" she never expressed it in her letters to her husband, but life was miserable for her. While he was traversing the Atlantic, she wrote him almost every day, with the knowledge that her letters would not be received until later and that he would not be able to send anything to her. She was fortunate to be able to stay with Hugh's brother Henry and his wife Henrietta while the ship crossed.

Ida was terribly lonely and scared of what might happen on the seas and after the ship landed. The newspapers recounted the bad news of German victories. She desperately wanted Hugh to be promoted to brigadier general so he would be further removed from the battleground, but a newspaper article named twenty-one officers who received that promotion, and her Hugh was not among them.

As time dragged on and there was no news of the ship landing, she felt that she could no longer impose on Henry and Henrietta, and so she moved with her sons to the Manhattan Square Hotel. There she had two rooms but was able to cook most meals for herself and her family, so she could save money by not eating the hotel meals. The nearby elevated train noisily roared by, day and night.

Finally, on May 1, she received a telegram that Hugh had landed in France, and the fear of the crossing at least was over. On May 18, she received her first letter and on May 26, five more. She was happy that Hugh was staying at the chateau in Bligny in comfortable surroundings.

In mid-May, she became aware that the allotment that Hugh had arranged from his salary was not being paid. She wrote and had friends talk with the Quartermaster's Depot in Washington, but the problem was not straightened out for a couple of months. She and her boys left the hotel and rejoined Henry and Henrietta and their family. As she put it, "I feel like a tramp." She was miserable, but never in her many letters to her husband did she ever question "why?"

FOUR

AMALGAMATION

THE AMERICAN TROOPS FIGHTING IN EUROPE WERE officially called the American Expeditionary Force (AEF). They were led by General John J. Pershing, who was appointed by President Woodrow Wilson with instructions to lead a separate American army and not permit his troops to be integrated, or "amalgamated," the term of the day, as individuals or groups into the depleted ranks of the other Allies. The French and British wanted amalgamation, believing that they had the experience to lead the Allies more quickly to victory, or stave off threatened loss, better than the disorganized and inexperienced Americans. Pershing wanted to build a distinctive army from top to bottom. He "was decidedly against our becoming a recruiting agency for either the French or British."[1]

There was a tactical reason for Pershing to insist that the Americans fight as a separate unit. He had observed the military stalemate of the previous three years where troops hunkered in trenches in close proximity to each other, but separated by entanglements of barbed wire and engaged in inconsequential raids preceded by heavy artillery fire. He thought that simply replacing troops to continue the same type warfare would not lead to a successful conclusion. Ignoring what was then considered modern warfare, Pershing wanted "open warfare," with the most important weapon being the rifle.[2] Pershing wrote, "Machine guns, grenades, Stokes mortars, and one-pounders . . . were all valuable weapons for specific purposes but could not replace the combination of an efficient soldier and his rifle."[3]

The conflict over amalgamation pitted the Allied generals and politicians against one another in occasionally rancorous and potentially destructive negotiations. President Wilson's "ultimate war aim was to influence the peace making following the war." "A policy of amalgamation might have obscured the American contribution to victory, whereas the effort of an independent American army was more discernible, more obvious."[4] Thus, the President demanded a separate and successful American army.

Negotiating for the Americans in the discussions with the other Allies was General Pershing, with instructions from Wilson as commander in chief not to amalgamate. Pershing, age fifty-seven, was a self-made man of the hardest sort. His grandfather had come to America from the Alsace-Lorraine area of France, with which both the general and Colonel Wise became very familiar during the war. The previous German spelling of Pershing's name had been anglicized.[5] John Pershing had been born in Missouri to a railroading family, in a railroad boardinghouse.[6] He started out as poor and ambitious. He gained appointment to West Point by acing a competitive exam sponsored by his local congressman. He distinguished himself at the academy and throughout his military career.

On a stint in Washington, D.C., he married Frankie, the daughter of influential Senator Francis E. Warren, thereby further advancing an already promising career. In 1916 and 1917, General Pershing led the American troops in their futile chase of the bandit Pancho Villa in Mexico. Adding to an inherent unhappiness, his wife and three daughters had died in a fire in 1915.

General Pershing got his nickname of "Black Jack," not because he was a poker player, although he proved to be astute in negotiations with fellow Allies; nor because his scowling visage, ramrod bearing, and sour demeanor resembled that weapon. He acquired the nickname because in Cuba he had commanded "colored" troops, as the blacks in the service were called at the time.

General Bullard, who knew Pershing from West Point, described his cadet days:

> Of regular but not handsome features and of robust, strong body, broad shouldered and well developed; almost or quite six feet tall; plainly of the estate of man while those about him were still boys; with keen searching gray eyes and intent look, Pershing inspired confidence but not affection. Personal magnetism seemed lacking. He won followers, but not personal worshippers. Plain in word, sane and direct in action, he applied himself to all duty and all work with a manifest purpose, not only succeeding in what he attempted, but of surpassing, guiding, and directing his fellows in what was before him. His exercise of authority, was then and always has been since, of a nature peculiarly impersonal, dispassionate, hard and firm.[7]

Of Pershing in France, Bullard later wrote, "Such was the man, as I saw him, that came to command the A.E.F. in Europe: ambitious, fit, intent upon his purpose, vigorous, firm, thoughtful, discreet, impersonal and dispassionate in requiring obedience."[8] Bullard and others also described the general as fiercely loyal and, to the consternation of many, "obstinate." On the personal side, Pershing was never short of female companionship and was devoted to his lover, Micheline Resco, whom he visited frequently in Paris during the war and eventually married many years later, shortly before his death.[9]

During most of the war, there had been a lack of coordination between the French and British. Pershing wrote, "First one and then the other would attack, each apparently without reference to the other."[10] He went on to say that the lack of coordination would allow the enemy to utilize its reserves against first one and then the other and that would never lead to victory. The French and British finally realized the problem and on March 26, 1918, at a joint conference at Doullens, French general Ferdinand Foch, age sixty-seven, was approved as Supreme Commander (in French, Marshal) of the Allied forces.[11] On April 3, the French, British, and Americans signed an agreement formalizing the appointment. The Marshal's job was to coordinate the deployment of the troops of each country.

Foch was a devout Catholic who had been schooled by the Jesuits and had personally watched as the Germans captured the French fortress town of Metz during the Franco-Prussian War of 1871. He had lost his son and son-in-law in the first year of the present war.[12] He was very learned in artillery warfare. He had served as head of the École de Guerre (School of War), had been a brilliant general in the first battle of the Marne, and had been chief of staff for French commander-in-chief Henri Philippe Pétain. He was picked for the position by French premier Georges Clémenceau because of his brains. He also represented "the passionate Gallic spirit."[13] The British supported his selection because he was more offensive-minded than Pétain.[14] Since the fall of Metz in the previous war, Foch had dedicated his life to revenge.[15]

Pétain, age sixty-two, was one of the few French leaders who were considered heroes by the French populace. He had been instrumental in fighting off the German attack at Verdun. It was he who quelled the troop mutinies of 1917, by judicious use of punishment and reforms to the harsh regimen of the French military service. Following the mutinies, he favored mostly defensive actions by the French troops with limited offensive forays. His strategy was to wait for the Americans and more French tanks. Like Pershing, with whom he became friends, he was blunt-spoken and extremely stubborn.[16]

Above Foch and Pétain in the French hierarchy was *Le Tigre*, Premier Georges Clémenceau, a short seventy-six-year-old bundle of energy.[17] Solitary and ill-tempered, he was given to displays of violent rage, punctuated by vituperative discourse. General Bullard described the premier as follows: "He came in midwinter—a plain, short, stocky man, with a heavy grayish moustache, and wearing very plain clothes. He was old, but carried his many years lightly. . . . His eye was clear and looked at you very straight. . . . His general look, I am sure, was not that which gave him the name of 'The Tiger.' It was kindly enough, yet certainly he had in his face something that suggested great firmness, ay, fierceness of purpose, a determination to fight for that purpose. It was a face that could be made hard, absolutely immovable."[18]

During a stint in America, he courted and married an American, but the marriage did not last long because he was impossible to live with. Long before the war, his wife and children retreated back to the United States. He was a fencer, and while in America had taught that dueling sport.[19] When General Bullard compared him to American general and later president Andrew Jackson because of their similar fierce, fighting determination, the Tiger retorted, "but I never fought a duel on horseback."[20]

In his politics, Clémenceau was anticlerical and liberal, and as a youth, had served a jail sentence for participation in a political riot.[21] As a politician, he was so difficult to accommodate that it is said that he was appointed premier because he made it impossible for anyone else to form a cabinet. He was as anticlerical as Foch was devoutly Catholic, but he was a realist. Above all, he wanted revenge on Germany after watching the Germans defeat of the French in 1871. He selected Foch, the best man for the job.

For the British there was commander-in-chief Sir Douglas Haig, age sixty, an aristocrat and favorite of King George V. He was hated, however, by British prime minister David Lloyd George, who regarded him as "reactionary and outdated" in his military leadership.[22] Haig came from a wealthy Scottish family, their land located for centuries on the border with England.[23] That family was constantly at war with either the English or its Scottish neighbors. He was dour, stubborn, and devout. Although he was not a strong academic student, he made up for his shortcomings by hard work. Throughout the war, Haig felt that he was a man on a mission. He attended church every Sunday during the war and wrote to his brother, "We are meant to win."[24]

Following British setbacks early in the war, General Haig had undermined and then replaced his predecessor and friend, General John French. He now aspired to be the savior of the British people, although his lack of success did not seem to have him on that road. Haig was a devotee of outdated cavalry charges. Addressing Britain's heavy losses in this war, he commented, "We lament too much over death."[25]

Historian Nick Lloyd describes the role of Marshal Foch as follows: "Despite his impressive-sounding brief, Foch's authority was limited, and crucially he could not order anyone to do anything. The full tactical control of Allied armies was left to their national commanders, who could appeal to their governments if they felt endangered by any of his instructions. But Foch could inspire and suggest, push and prod. His position meant that he could take a wider view of the war, above and beyond mere national contingents."[26]

The issue of amalgamation first arose with the problem of how to transport the American troops to France. The Americans, even with the German ships that they had seized, did not have the capacity to transport the number of men needed to win the war. The British had the ships, but to make them available for troops would require sacrificing the shipping of essential goods to the already-strapped island. Prime Minister Lloyd George had a solution: If British ships were to be used as troop transports, then they would transport infantry and machine-gun men to serve in the British ranks.[27] The French, not to be outdone, but without ships, demanded the same type and number of American soldiers to fill their ranks. The Americans replied that was not acceptable. To the Americans, the British ships would carry full divisions with all the necessary supplies to be self-sufficient.

On January 29, 1918, the dispute was supposedly resolved with the Six Division Plan, whereby the British would transport six divisions to serve on the British front. The British and the Americans, however, interpreted the agreement differently. The British received six full divisions, including support personnel, not just soldiers. The British, who wanted only soldiers to fill their depleted ranks, not support personnel and supplies, were angry.

The situation on the front took a sharp turn for the worse. On March 21, 1918, the Germans launched their expected spring offensive. Initially, it was very successful, especially against the British, whose lines were pushed back thirty-seven miles, threatening the important railroad center at Amiens.[28] The British 5th Army was decimated: 212,000 British soldiers were killed or wounded and 90,000 prisoners were taken.[29] The generals panicked. On March 28, Pershing told Foch that all American troops would be made available to Foch to be used as he thought best.[30] Furthermore, infantry and machine gunners were to have priority on the British transports.[31] The formation of the separate American army would have to wait.

The 5th Division, of which the 61st Infantry commanded by Colonel Wise was a part, was one of the divisions to be sent as soon as possible.[32] On April 8, it arrived at Camp Merritt, awaiting American, not British, transportation. The following day, the Germans began a serious attack near Ypres on the Lys River. That offensive was still active, reaching its conclusion when the 61st Infantry disembarked in Brest on April 28. That attack, which resulted in 146,000 Allied troops wounded or dead, was called off by the Germans at the end of April, fortunately without attaining its original goals.[33]

While the 61st Infantry settled into training, the Allies continued to negotiate among themselves about how to use the American troops and whether there should even be a separate American army. Finally, at Abbeville, on May 2, 1918, the Allies reached an agreement. At that meeting, according to Pershing's account, Marshal Foch challenged him, "Are you willing to risk our being driven back to the Loire?" To which Pershing replied, "Yes, I am willing to take that risk."[34] Foch does not describe such brinkmanship.[35] To the teller belongs the tale.

At Abbeville, an agreement was reached that an American army would be formed as quickly as possible. But, to meet the present emergency, American troops would be transported to France as soon as could be arranged, with preference for infantry and machine gunners, who were to be trained and placed in service with the British and French armies at the discretion of General Pershing, after consultation with Marshal Foch.[36] Although Pershing apparently prided himself in refusing to capitulate, in reality, the question of amalgamation was kicked down the road, waiting to be resolved at a later date. The devilish details would be worked out in the future by consultation between Pershing and Foch.

By prearrangement, the 61st Infantry would be trained by the French. The instruction was to be done in three stages: (1) practice in use of weaponry; (2) a month's tour in the trenches by smaller units with French regiments; (3) then into trenches with their own American officers, but as a unit of a French corps.[37]

On the day of the Abbeville agreement, the Lead Soldier wrote:

Chateau de Bligny, Champagne, 2 May 18
Dear Hugh,
My last letter ended just as we were getting ready to go to sleep on the train night before last.

* * *

All day we joggled through the beautiful country. The war has not swept over that part of France and on that beautiful May Day we might have been able to forget that there is a war except for the great trainloads of troops and war material going our way and the field hospital trains coming from the other direction. Also we frequently passed gangs of Boche prisoners working on the track or in the freight yards.

Now, if you will look at the map you will see, about a hundred miles east by south from Paris, a town called Bar-Sur-Aube that is where we detrained today. The Sphinx told us last night that we should arrive at our destination at 11:00 a.m. but early this morning we pulled in.

Bar-Sur-Aube is not a large city and its station is a small one but a few minutes after our arrival it was a busy one.

Immediately, the troops were off, rifles were stacked, equipment was piled, and details were unloading the train and loading the trucks.

Meantime, the Colonel went to division headquarters to report the arrival of the regiment and to receive orders.

This is what is called a training area—where troops just arrived from the United States are put through a period of intensive training before going into the lines.

Our full division is to be in this vicinity.

Our regimental headquarters will be at Bligny, about 5 miles from Bar-Sur-Aube and the regiment will be billeted there and in neighboring towns and villages which, in France, are much closer to each other than they are at home. You know, in our country the villages are quite distances apart and the country is scattered over with farmhouses. But here one rarely sees a separate farmhouse.

The farmers live in villages and go out to their farms to work. So, there is a town or a village every mile or two along the roads.

This makes possible the method of sheltering troops without camping. They are "billeted" in the towns and villages.

Every town in France is listed for the number of troops it can accommodate and the "Town Major" of the locality, a French officer or non-commissioned officer, keeps data as to how many men or officers each house in his district can be made to take in, without moving the inhabitants. The law requires the people to take in that number and they are paid a fixed rate.

The men are usually billeted in the public buildings, the factories, barns, etc. and sleep in their own blankets on straw. The officers have rooms in some private residence. The government pays a franc a day for an officer's billet, the officer paying a little in addition for his sheets and towels. When troops move to a locality they are preceded by a billeting party consisting usually of the regimental billeting officer, an officer of each battalion and a non-commissioned officer of each company. They arrange with the Town Major and assign the billets so, when the troops arrive, they can lead the organizations right to their new quarters.

As soon as arrangements were all made for unloading the train and for sending of the property to the billets, the majors were assembled and given their instructions. Then the Colonel with his Adjutant and two other staff officers got into an automobile and drove to Bligny where the regimental billeting officer met them, reporting most satisfactory arrangements as having been made for the regiment.

Also, we were met by Monsieur Le Maire (The Mayor) and after he and the Colonel had gone through with customary formalities and had told each other how proud each was of being the ally of the other, etc., etc., etc., we were driven to our billet and I wish you could see it!

We drove in through a big iron gate, along a winding driveway, up the hill through a beautiful park and stopped in front of the magnificent Chateau de Bligny.

"Here's your billet sir!" said the billeting officer. "What! This shanty?" replied the Colonel—"Is this the best you could do for your Colonel?—Oh well! It will do—C'est la guerre."

Just then the carved oak door swung open and a large handsome man, past middle age, came out and with a courtly bow, offered his hand: "Ahh, mon Colonel! Welcome to my humble

NORTHWEST EUROPE
WESTERN FRONT
1918

0   10   20   30   40   50
SCALE IN MILES

home which is quite all yours so long as our American allies wish it."

Then he led us through the handsome halls, all decorated with stag's heads and boar's heads, to the room assigned as billets for the Colonel, the Lieutenant Colonel and the Adjutant. They were all fine but I shall just describe the Colonel's; it is about 25 feet square, with upholstered walls and hardwood floors covered with skins on Oriental rugs. The furniture is of inlaid ebony and the bed is a kind of mountain of luxury. There is a large open fireplace with onyx mantle and a huge gilt framed mirror and an adjoining closet with hot and cold water—now did you ever hear of starting off in a war like this?

But the most beautiful thing about our billet is the outlook from the great windows over the rolling hills of Champagne covered with their sun-gilded vineyards.

No wonder they call the champagne from these vineyards "bottled sunshine."

We followed the Baron down to his library where we met his family and then went to the dining hall for a wonderful luncheon. It was kind of an official occasion so only the men were present.

By the time luncheon was over, the troops were arriving and the remainder of the day was busy getting them all settled.

By the time night came, I guess the Colonel was good and ready for that big soft bed and he took me out of the dispatch case, set me on the mantle and tumbled in.

Good night,
Your Soldier

The next letter written by the Lead Soldier covered several days.

10 May 18
Dear Hugh,

We have been at Bligny all week and we are beginning to feel like old inhabitants.

It is a quaint little town nestled in a valley with the vine-covered hills above it. The narrow streets wind and twist like cow paths which, originally, no doubt they were. The picturesque little stone houses are so small that they make the great chateau which dominates the town from its hill all the more imposing.

The hillsides of the beautiful surrounding country are covered with vineyards and the more level or rolling stretches are grain fields and pastures. Here and there are big tracts of forest where there are deer and wild boar.

There are fine herds of cows but one cannot get butter nor milk because all the milk is used for making cheese and, furthermore, their methods of handling milk would never pass our milk inspectors.

In the woods Boche prisoners are kept at work getting out timber which goes up to the front to be used in the entrenchments and some are employed in the vineyards. A detachment of them are quartered here and seem friendly enough but the Colonel does not allow anyone to speak to them.

Regimental headquarters and the special companies are here but the battalions are in neighboring towns where each has its own maneuver ground, practice trenches and target range. Occasionally they assemble here for a review or for a "march past." At the last of these, a day or so ago, the Colonel gave the right of line to a French company which is here demonstrating their attack formations. They were very much pleased at this honor and it was an inspiring occasion for our men to be in line with these veterans of many battles.

Our training schedule requires 8 hours a day of intensive work and as the Colonel sees the entire regiment at work every day he is as busy as they are. He now has his car so he can get around but at first he had to go on a motorcycle or in a hired cart.

Our regimental headquarters mess is now running. The mess officer found a little restaurant in town that has everything necessary except food so we hired the building and equipment, put in our cooks, and started housekeeping.

Once a week the YMCA comes to one of billet towns and gives a movie show and the Colonel sends the band around to give concerts. Sunday afternoon it plays at the chateau where all the officers come to a sort of informal reception of Madame La Baron. She is very sweet and considerate and seems to feel very tenderly towards the young officers for her only son, a lieutenant of the dragoons, was recently killed in battle.

It is so beautiful, so comfortable, so quiet here that we could hardly realize how close we are to the war were it not for the strenuous training that keeps its purpose ever in our minds. Then, too, at night we can often see the dim red flashes against the sky and sometimes we hear the muffled boom of the guns way off to the North.

* * *

26 May 18

I laid my letter aside two weeks ago and I have been too busy dashing around with the Colonel in his car or jogging around in his dispatch case on horseback to finish it.

Things are fairly humming here for they need us badly at the front and our training must be rushed. Last night a message came that General Pershing would inspect the regiment today and there was some tall hustling to have the troops ready for him on his arrival.

When the General's automobile drove into Bligny the troops were formed along the Main Street and looked very business like in their steel helmets and it was easy to see the improvement that has taken place in the past month.

Here, in the sound of the guns, the men all realize what serious work is ahead of them and they work earnestly to learn their parts in the great game they are soon to play.

When the General had passed around the troops he halted and faced the Colonel, he said: "Do you consider you are ready to go in?" "Yes Sir, and we are anxious to go in" replied the Colonel. "Your regiment looks good—you will not be held back long" said the general as he stepped into his car.

June 1

Such a bustle as we have had today. All our equipment and field baggage was sent to the train and loaded on and then the regiment marched to Brienne Le Chateau where it is in training.

Brienne Le Chateau is where Napoleon went to school, but beyond that it is not very interesting—not so for us because we arrived in the night and we will pull out before day.

Even the Colonel does not know this time where we are going—"Just up front"—that's all. But that is enough to make us all very happy. It cannot be much longer now before we have our throw at the Boche.

June 2

Just before day this morning we slid out of the yards at Brienne, the regiment in four long trains and today we have puffed and toiled up grade North.

There is nothing remarkable about our departure except the order and quietness of it all. About the only difficulty we had was with the Colonel's automobile. There was no ramp to load it over and the French railway officer decided to send it on the next day—"Not Much!" said the Colonel, "I want that when we get there!"—Whereupon he called over a company that was standing waiting to entrain and they lifted the car bodily onto a flat car.

All afternoon we wound up the steep fir-covered mountains and at about sunset a staff officer came aboard and gave the Colonel the orders showing where we are going.

Headquarters and one battalion to go to Gerardmer and the other battalions to places near there.

We are coming close to Gerardmer now and close to the front, too, for we can hear the boom of the guns and they have not that distant muffled sound we heard occasionally in Champagne.

Good night,
Your Soldier

While the 61st Infantry was in training in the Bar-sur-Aube area, on May 27, 1918, the Germans began a massive assault on the French position northeast of Paris on the Aisne River at Chemin des Dames. This was to be their way to Paris and the end of the war. On the first day of the assault 5,300 guns opened fire, spewing two million shells. Shortly thereafter, the Germans crossed the Aisne and reached the river Marne. They fired their long-range guns, Big Berthas, on Paris, then only forty miles away.[38]

On May 28, troops of the American 1st Division, commanded by General Bullard and attached to the French army, scored the first American victory of the war when they captured the town of Cantigny and held it against bloody counterattacks.[39] In early June, the American 2nd and 3rd divisions, which Pershing had provided to a desperate Pétain, won bitterly fought victories in Chateau-Thierry and Belleau Wood.[40] Those battles were to the north of the 5th Division and its 61st Infantry. They were won by the most experienced American divisions, which were attached to, but not amalgamated into, the French army. Now, it was clear that the Americans were to be a factor in the war.

New American troops were coming to France in great numbers. From March through June the arrivals increased from 64,000 to 238,000 per month.[41] Regardless of how the Americans were deployed, or by whom they were trained, the Germans could not possibly keep up.

FIVE

THE VOSGES, THE NOT-SO-QUIET SECTOR

AS THE LEAD SOLDIER HAD POINTED OUT, BEFORE THE war Gérardmer had been a resort town in the Vosges, a low-lying mountain range extending along the border between France and Germany to Switzerland. Both France and Germany considered the area unsuitable for major offensives and, thus, it came to be considered "a semi-quiet sector." In close proximity to each other, opposing troops dug in and lived in trenches, occasionally pestering each other with small local attacks. Gérardmer was sufficiently out of the way that it was not much affected by the warfare and was an excellent base for training.

Once again, the Colonel got lucky with his accommodations. The Lead Soldier wrote:

Gerardmer
3 June 18
Dear Hugh,
    Last night, as we pulled into the station here, the booming of the guns had increased to a steady roar only a few miles away.

In other wars I suppose it would have been called a battle that was going on but, in this war, they say just: "Oh, it's nothing special—just one of the regular bombardments"—several times a day the artillery on one side or the other showers the other fellow's position.

This is called a semi-quiet sector but you would not think it is semi-quiet if you could hear it.

When we arrived, the French Town Mayor took off the billeting parties and, when we had detrained, the troops followed them. Then the Colonel, Lieutenant Colonel and Adjutant went to their billets in the hotel La Providence—Well! We have had a royal suite, a stable, a castle and now we have a summer resort for our home. The other staff officers are billeted in a handsome villa which is also the regimental headquarters.

Our hotel is running and is full of guests, mainly French and Russian officers, but the Colonel prefers to keep up the headquarters mess so the mess officer has hired the kitchen and dining staff of a hotel across the street from us.

Today we received orders attaching our regiment to a French corps whose headquarters is here and the Colonel went to report to the corp commander. I think he was much surprised when the corp commander told him we were needed in the line at once and that our final training period would have to be cut to a minimum for we should be in the line in ten days, at the outside.

"How do you feel about it?" asked the General—"Are your men ready?" "We are green," replied the Colonel, "But we are eager to get in. Our willingness will help make up for lack of experience—you can trust us."

The General sent for the colonel in charge of training and directed him to cooperate with our Colonel. They have been together all day going over training grounds and preparing schedules while the troops are settling themselves and policing their billets. It is quite evident from the amount of cleaning up we do that our ideas of sanitation differ materially from the ideas of the troops that precede us.

Gerardmer is a lovely little city nestled in a valley in the high Vosges mountains beside an exquisite clear blue lake. Before the war it was a famous summer and winter resort and it is full of handsome villas and fine new hotels, most of which are now used for military purposes.

The country is typically Swiss in appearance—beautiful blue lakes fill the valleys between the high fir clad mountains the lower slopes of which are green with the rich pastures. Here and there on the pasture lands are picturesque little chalets and dairies for here cheese is what grapes were in Champagne.

There is an immense Caserne (barracks) here where French troops from the front are rested and replaced and put in condition to return to the fight and there are contingents of troops of several other nations.

There is a battalion of Russians who are being organized, they having left Russia and refused to live under the present Russian government. There are British troops, Canadian troops, Italians, and even Anamites, from Indo-China. All these races and colors are bent on just one purpose—whipping the Boche but, after four years, he is still not whipped.

It is surprising how business goes on here. Only 17 kilometers behind the front lines, the stores and markets are open and show little signs of war but nearly every day Boche avions come over and then there is a show with the anti-aircraft batteries in the hills surrounding the towns.

One of these performances took place today. A couple of Boche planes came over to reconnoiter. All over town the bugles blew and everyone darted into the nearest house not only to prevent the Boche seeing what is in town but also to get out of the way of falling fragments of the shells fired at the planes. We are pretty close to the real show now, Hukins, things are livening up—10 days more and then what?

Good night,

Your Soldier

The Colonel's excitement about getting to the front was not reciprocated in New York City, where Ida continued to have a rough go of it. Her concern for her husband was not her only worry. By mid-June, her monthly allotment had still not been started despite inquiries and complaints by her and the Colonel. That allotment had been requested and the paperwork completed in March.

New York City did not seem safe from the war. On June 3, Ida wrote that the newspapers had reported the submarine sinking of a ship off the New Jersey coast. Destroyers were after the culprit, but success in finding the quarry was doubtful. People feared an aerial attack launched from submarines, a far-fetched threat, but enough for the authorities to ask people to turn off their lights at night. Times Square was dark and Broadway at night was deserted. Anti-aircraft guns were placed on top of tall buildings. It seemed to Ida that the Germans were trying to "terrorize" the city.

Her concern for her husband, however, was paramount. On June 15, she wrote, "I wonder when the 61st will be sent forward. Do write me or cable me whatever you can. If I knew you would be kept in training another month, it would be such a comfort, but I imagine you are sent further forward, perhaps by now, and I am miserable." She did not know where he was, whether he was in the fighting, or even if he was alive. She only knew what had been true two or three weeks before when she had received his last letter. With fear, she read the casualty reports in the newspapers and any news at all about troop movements. She fervently hoped that the Colonel would be promoted to brigadier general so that he could be even more removed from the fighting, or reassigned away from the front, or even better, sent home to train others.

She was also concerned about his bad leg. She sent him adhesive bandages and medicines which she hoped would reach him and would help. He had not written about how he was doing with that ailment. He seldom wrote anything personal about himself.

Rather than resort housing, Ida was looking at subsistence. She wrote, "I went to see Miss Momword's rooms today. They are big and airy, but that's all that is pleasant about them. Gas, no electricity, a painted tin bathtub which is so rough. Shabby, dingy old furniture and carpets literally full of holes." For $27 per week, she was reluctant to have her children play on carpets that had been tromped on by generations of Momwords and had not decided what to do. For now, she and the boys were staying at the home of her generous in-laws, Henry and Henrietta, while they were away. When they returned, rather than impose, she decided to return home, to Watertown, New York, for the month of July where they could stay with other relatives.

The Colonel had concealed his bum leg, but he had quietly consulted an eminent New York orthopedist before he left for France. General Pershing made it clear that he wanted young healthy officers.[1] "He (Pershing) is looking for results. He intends to have them. He will sacrifice any man who does not bring them."[2] Pershing, however, had been very complimentary of the Colonel and his command when inspecting at Bligny. During that visit, the Colonel had successfully hidden his problem. He never spoke easily of it. The usually informative Lead Soldier never made mention of a leg problem. Finally, at the insistence of Ida, in a letter to her on June 12, the Colonel opened up:

> The reason I have not told you more of my health is that there has been nothing to tell. I have been comfortable all the time and luxurious part of the time. With the exception of one thing, of which you know, I am in perfect health and I hope and try to believe that it is better. I have to save it and camouflage it and it is the source of constant apprehension and mental anguish but I get around as lively as any colonel I know. It is an awful handicap but I have been in races before with handicap and I'll see it through. I never in my life felt more energetic, confident and competent and if it were not for that hold-back, I do not know whether the regiment could hold my gait.

In many places, such as the Vosges, the troops had dug trenches by hand and shovel. There was no machinery to help, and the trenches were not like those built in Cuba. Troops on both sides lived and fought in those trenches, protected by thick brambles of almost impenetrable barbed wire. Wire cutters, grenades, and poisonous gas, all lacking in flamboyant appeal, became essential tools of battle. Long-range artillery was crucial to try to clear the barbed wire and soften resistance before foot soldiers "went over the top," leaving their trenches to invade those of the enemy, hopefully capturing the latter with short-range gunfire and the dreaded bayonet. That murderous blade made killing intimate and death graphic.

General Pershing thought that war should be fought with rifles and won by superior marksmanship.[3] His British and French peers thought that naïve. It was not very effective to sharpshoot an occasional venturer outside a trench. Machine guns killed in multiples. Disputing how the war should be fought naturally led to disputing how, as well as by whom, training should be conducted. For the 61st Infantry, assigned to the Vosges sector and to be trained by the French, trench warfare was the main course, but American marksmanship was also mandatory. The Lead Soldier wrote:

Gerardmer 12 June 18
Dear Hugh,

We have had our 10 days of final training and they have been real training with no restriction on expenditure of material and ammunition. This area has been prepared by the French for the training of their troops and has all the necessary maneuver grounds, target ranges, practice trenches, grenade pits and paraphernalia. About the only thing that is not adequate are the target ranges for the French do not seem to attach as much importance to individual rifle fire as we do. Whatever else we teach the men, we always impress them with the fact that the rifle with its bayonet is the infantry weapon which is to win the war and that his other weapons are accessories.

So, we have put up long lines of small targets near each battalion billets and near them lines of dummies for bayonet practice. Each day every man fires his allotted number of shots—slow fire, rapid fire—magazine fire and fire with its gas mask on. Also he attacks and punches and slashes the dummies with his bayonet.

While part of the company is doing these things another part is firing with the automatic rifles, another is shooting rifle grenades and another bombing through the trenches. Then the company is assembled and put through combat formations and practice assaults combining all these specialties and companies are brought together for battalion tactical work.

Meanwhile the headquarters company is having a circus of its own—the 37 mm platoon bangs away with its wonderful little guns, the Stokes mortar platoon tosses its high explosive shells, the Pioneer platoon is making entanglements, digging trenches, building dugouts. The Signal platoon is working with its wireless, its ground telegraphs, its telegraph and telephone apparatus, flags, flares and lanterns.

Off up the valley one can hear the buzz of the machine company practicing with its Maxims.

From sunrise to sunset it sounds like a battle and often when there is a lull in our own racket, we can hear the distant growl of the real fight for which we are rehearsing.

So have our 10 days been spent in hard serious work preparing ourselves for the great game we are about to enter.

After work hours there is a lot of fun for both the officers and the men who have entered into the spirit of comraderie with our allies. Our band plays every afternoon on the square which then looks like a congress of nations and several nights a week it plays as orchestra as the soldiers' casino in a big theater where there is a soldier vaudeville.

One day the manager of this casino asked our amusement officer if he could furnish a few numbers for the program. "Yes, he replied, "The whole program if you wish us to"; and since then, we have been furnishing most of the show.

**

Just as we did at Bligny, the regiment has made friends here and our only difficulty has been with the Russians. Parties of them were in the habit of swaggering about town bullying the Frenchmen they met. One evening they tried it on our men and learned to their sorrow what handy men Americans are with their fists. The Russian guard came to rescue their comrades and our men took away their rifles and ran them out of town.

The old man was much mortified over this occurrence, though he thoroughly sympathized with the men, I am sure, so he went up to the Caserne to apologize to the French commander but the latter said "*Ne parlez pas de cela, monsieur Colonel, je suis enchanté—merci.*" ("Don't speak of that, my Colonel, I am delighted, thank you.")

Ever since we have been here there have been almost daily fracases between the Boche planes and the French archies (anti-aircraft guns) on the surrounding hills. Evidently, Fritz wants to know what is going on here and Frenchie is determined that he shall not have a look.

A day or so ago, the Colonel's curiosity got the better of him and he decided to visit one of the batteries which had been especially active. They started early so as to be there when the day cleared and visibility was good—the time the Boche usually arrive. We went most of the way in the car and then horseback up to the battery on top of the mountain. Oh! Such a panorama as spread out below us—the beautiful country, the picturesque towns, the exquisite lakes! But there was not much time to enjoy scenery for, hardly had we arrived when the lookout shouted: "Avion qui vient du Nord." ("Airplane that comes from the North.") And there it was—a shiny speck approaching through the blue sky! Instantly every man was at his post—the gunners jumped down into the circular pits where the guns were—the pointers and loaders mounted the carriages behind the gun shields. The turner of the wheel spun the gun carriages around til the muzzles pointed towards the approaching speck and another turn elevated the muzzle. All around the pit, instruments were clicking off measurements of angles, wind velocity, speed of the planes, etc. etc. and were computing automatically the firing data. All the time the gunner was holding his sights on the approaching speck.

Larger and larger it grew—then we could see the wings—then the men between the wings and Bang! Whirr! Boom! A puff of fleecy white smoke appeared above the plane—Bang! Whirr! Boom!—Another puff below him! Another! Another! Another! Another! Another and still the plane seemed to be leaving a trail of white fleece balls to mark its path across the cloudless sky.

But they were coming too close for Heinie's (slang for German) comfort and he tried to turn and rise—too late! One of the puffs appeared right in front of him—His right wing crumpled and flew upward. The plane turned upside down and shot like a plummet thousands of feet into the valley below.

What a cheer went up from the battery! The men of the crew put the gunpointer on their shoulders and galloped around the pit til they were dizzy. He'll get a Croix, that fellow!

Good night,

Your Soldier

At last, it was time to get to the front, the trenches a short distance southeast of the town of St. Dié. The 61st Infantry was attached to the French 21st Division d'Infanterie, XI Corps d'Armée. On June 15, the very day when Ida wrote that she wondered if the 61st had been sent forward, the Lead Soldier wrote:

15 June 18

Dear Hugh,

The afternoon of June 11, the orders came for us to move into position by battalions at one day intervals. The Colonel selected the Third Battalion to lead the regiment into the line in the Violu and La Cude subsector of the Anould sector. The First

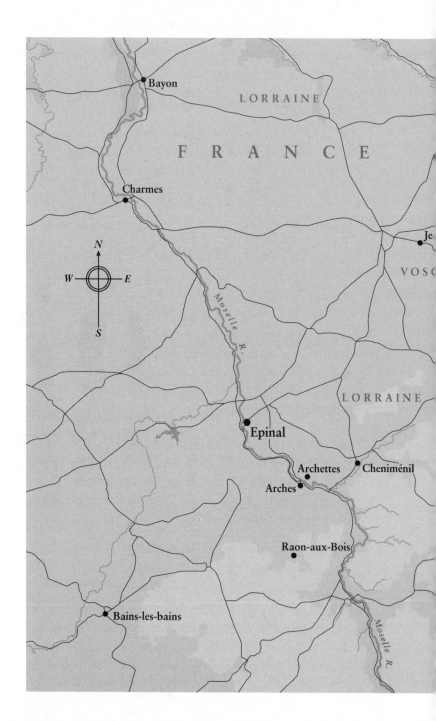

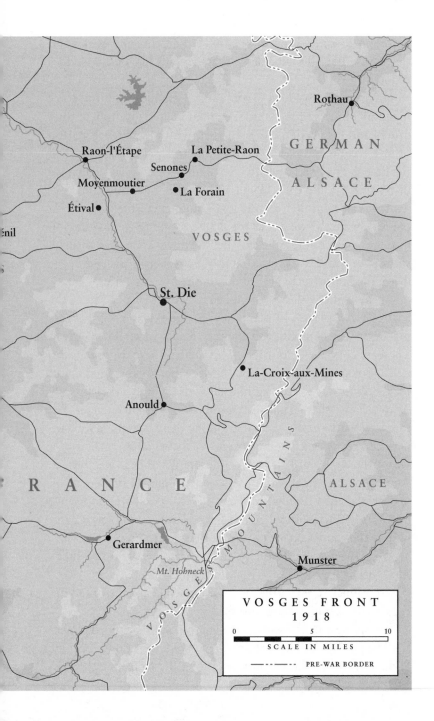

Rothau

GERMAN

Raon-l'Étape   La Petite-Raon   ALSACE

Senones

Moyenmoutier   La Forain

Étival

Énil   VOSGES

St. Die

La-Croix-aux-Mines

Anould

FRANCE   ALSACE

Gerardmer

Munster

Mt. Hobneck

VOSGES MOUNTAINS

**VOSGES FRONT
1918**

0   5   10

SCALE IN MILES

– – – – –   PRE-WAR BORDER

Battalion goes into support position at La Croix aux Mines and the Second Battalion in reserve. That sounds like business, does it not!

Having assembled the battalion commanders and the commanding officers of the special companies and given them their orders and instructions, the Colonel, with their French liaison officer, went to Anould to hold a conference at headquarters of the French division to which we will now be attached. Then we drove to Brial, the P.C. (Command Post) of our subsector.

It was a beautiful drive and it got more interesting as we went on; for the nearer we got to the Boche the more we saw the immediate results of the fighting. The first towns we passed through showed only a few damaged houses but towards the end of the drive, the houses were almost demolished by shell fire.

As we came within a few miles of La Croix aux Mines the road was, in places, in plain view of the Boche and, in those places, it was camouflaged by high fences of waddled brush. These, of course, do not prevent his seeing where the road is but he cannot see the road nor can he see what is passing along it. He therefore has to content himself with shelling it occasionally on the chance that he may catch something passing along it. But this is enough to make one hurry along these stretches. We happened to reach one when Fritz was chancing a few shells and it was rather awkward to have to decide whether it was best to stop or to open the throttle. We stopped a minute or so to think it over and then decided to "run it"—it is well we did for we had hardly started on when a big shell landed and blew a great hole in the road right where we had been standing.

We arrived at Brial hungry and just in time for a fine lunch (dejeuner) with the French regimental mess.

After lunch, the Colonel and the French Colonel worked out the details of our coming into the line.

We are new at the game so it is arranged that our regiment shall be sandwiched in with the French regiment till we become familiar with trench warfare. So, along the front line trenches we will alternate in combat groups (GCs) with the French. The Colonel and the French Colonel will have the PCs together and the commander of the front line battalion will be with the French Major and the captains and lieutenants will be with their own sections and groups in the line alongside the French groups. The French troops will be at once withdrawn from the support and reserve positions and, later, we will relieve them in the line.

While we were at lunch the Boche got quite disagreeable but no one minded his shells because we were well underground.

You will not find Brial on the map. It is not a town but just a name given the command post of this subsector. It is nothing more nor less than a row of dugouts in the hillside right up at the top of the Vosges mountains about ten miles from Saint Dié. From the little town of La Croix aux Mines you begin to leave the valley and to climb the mountain which separates German Alsace from French Alsace. Most of the road is concealed from Boche view by the heavy fir forest and where it is not concealed it is camouflaged. Just before you reach the crest you come to a place where there is a most wonderful view of the open rolling country and fertile fields in the valley below and, on the left side of the road at this point, you see the doors of the dugouts of the PC Brial where the commanding officer and his staff live under the ground to avoid shells as gophers do to avoid hawks. You would hardly notice this place for only the doors set back in the hillsides show. The fronts of the dwellings are just as nature made them and trees grow from their roofs. About 200 yards further up, you come upon more of these prairie dog dwellings extending all along the crest of the mountain where live the officers and the men of the centers of resistance (CRS) and a little way beyond them, are the front lines with their dugouts for the GCs.

Connecting all these trenches and dugouts are the communication trenches and the covered ways which enable these cave dwellers to move about the position unseen and protected from the Boche whose front line is but 30 to 70 meters from ours.

After these arrangements had been made we drove rapidly back to where the Third Battalion was bivouacking at the end of its first day's march and then on into Gerardmer.

Yesterday the First Battalion marched from Gerardmer, bivouacking where the Third Battalion had halted the night before, and the Second Battalion passed through Gerardmer following about ten kilometers behind the First. The machine gun company is with the Third Battalion and the headquarters company is also on the march. The supply company is changing its supply dumps from Gerardmer to La Croix aux Mines.

This should give you an idea of how a regiment moves. They change like this—it does not jump like a flea nor fly like a beetle—it moves like a measuring worm—first it raises its head and stretches forward and then brings its tail up to its head.

While all this is going on, you may be sure the Colonel and his staff are busy seeing that the head goes down in the right place, that the tail is pulled up to it, and that the long body is not disjointed nor tangled.

Yesterday the Third Battalion reached a point beyond which it was inadvisable to march by daylight so there they halted and waited for dark when the Boche could not see them nor the column of dust they raise in marching. From there, too, the march is made in column of platoons each separated from the next by 100 yards or more so that shelling or bombing might not catch a large body of troops.

The men are not allowed to smoke and greatest possible silence is maintained. If an avion approaches the men leave the road and lie down in the grass or brush til it has gone by. If there is any light, troops are particularly visible on the white roads and their shadows, when standing, show up very plainly to an aeroplane.

Creeping along this way the Third Battalion passed through La Croix aux Mines after dark and then to them came the task of entering the lines unobserved for, if a Fritz discovers a relief in progress, he will open with every gun in range and catch the troops in the midst of changing.

During the day the Major, with his captains and some lieutenants and non-commissioned officers of each company had gone ahead and reconnoitered the positions into which the organizations were to go.

As the head of each company arrived at the foot of the mountain, its captain met it and divided it into combat groups and supports for his section of the line and to each of those he assigned a guide that reconnoitered with him that day the position.

Each group moved off quietly to its position and there relieved the French troops who were holding there.

Each old group left two men with the new group to explain the situation to the newcomers and each new group sent a man to the group on each side of it for liaison.

It was all done so quietly that evidently the Boche did not suspect that a relief was in progress. There was only the normal amount of firing and we did not lose a man.

The Colonel stood out in the road at his PC listening and awaiting reports which came in regularly and, finally, an hour before dawn, he sent word to the French Colonel "the relief is complete—without incident."

The French Colonel was greatly pleased and sent a reply: "If your regiment can do that in its first operation, you have nothing to fear mon cher colonel."

So, today we are established in our positions.

The regimental office is at La Croix aux Mines but the Colonel has a forward combat headquarters up here at his PC where he stays being connected with La Croix aux Mines by telephone and motorcycle orderlies.

We've had considerable firing and shelling today for we are in the front lines and we are at last in the fight.

The Colonel has been plodding around through his centers of resistance, support points, and combat groups all day and is happy as a clam at high tide.

We have lived like a prince, like a baron, and now we are going to live like a rat.

Good Night,
Your Soldier

The next two days the men settled into their rat's maze of trenches, which had varying degrees of comfort and danger. The Lead Soldier wrote:

16 June 18
Dear Hugh,

The Boche was very disagreeable today—he must be peeved at us for coming into his front yard without letting him know about it or, perhaps, we have been rude to him today.

This morning he started out being quite friendly all along our front, calling out from his trenches and trying to engage our men in conversation. The Colonel had absolutely forbidden all fraternizing so Fritz's attempts at friendliness met cold rebuff.

At one point, where the lines are only 30 yards apart, Fritz tossed over packages of cigarettes to our men but when this was reported to our bad-mannered Colonel he ordered grenades returned for the cigarettes and then he ordered our whole line to snipe any Boche that showed himself. This ended all friendliness and the rest of the day both sides have been sniping continuously. Also, the Boche artillery has indulged itself in considerable strafing of our trenches.

If the Boche allows himself to be nagged into a game of give and take with us, he will be playing our game for he is no match for the American in daring, cunning, nor marksmanship.

The Colonel seems to be determined to worry Fritz—he has orders to poke him, nag him, and make his life as uncomfortable as possible. If he persists in his plan and continues as he has today, this will promptly cease to be a "semi-quiet" sector.

While the sector was held by a comparatively weak force, the French could not afford to expend strength on it but now, with the American reinforcement, the division commander heartily concurs in the policy of stirring things up a bit.

Today, the Colonel was through some of the forward GC's and everywhere he found the men carrying out his aggressive ideas with the utmost zeal and they were thoroughly enjoying the game.

In each group, a man was watching through a periscope while others stood ready with their rifles near the loopholes.

And such tricks are used to conceal these loopholes!—an old tomato can, apparently carelessly thrown out of the trench may be the opening through which the bullet will whiz if Fritz exposes himself. An old pair of breeches may cover the slit in the parapet where a sharp shooter is awaiting his chance. Sometimes a sniper may be out at the end of a little trench leading forward from the main trench or he may be camouflaged up in a tree. One of our best sniper posts is in an innocent looking stump which stands closer to the Boche than to us. The stump is hollow and a tunnel leads out to it and under it. A sniper stands in the bottom of the tunnel with his head up in the stump and watches through a slit in the bark.

The Boche is up to the same tricks—one of his most annoying posts turned out to be in an old sandbag which lay out in "no man's land."

So anything that looks as though it might possibly conceal a lookout or a sniper is occasionally riddled, on the chance that it is being so used.

The sniper is often so cleverly concealed that he is not even suspected till "ping" comes his bullet when someone exposes himself and he will lie quiet for hours awaiting his chance. So, there are many clever tricks for locating him—several men watch through periscopes while a dummy is exposed to tempt a sniper. When he shoots he may disclose his hiding place. A cardboard box dressed in a coat and helmet is raised over the parapet. The sniper puts a hole through it and then the periscope placed behind the hole will look straight to where the bullet came from.

You must not imagine that the front line trench is filled all its length with men. Rather, it is a narrow ditch connecting the positions of the combat groups, separated 25 yards or more and carefully prepared for defense and provided with dugouts.

Leading back from the front trenches to the trenches of the supports are the communication trenches or "Boyeaux" dug zig-zagged to prevent "enfilade" and all through the trenches there are "traverses" or jut outs so that a shell bursting in one place can do no damage far from that spot.

In front of the trenches are wire entanglements and all manner of traps and obstacles to prevent the approach of the enemy.

A trip through the trenches is no joke—zigzagging, winding, turning, twisting along the steep hillsides—stumbling and slipping on the narrow, oozy trench bottoms. Sometimes one can crawl in comparative safety but, in places he has to crouch or crawl to avoid the sharp vision of the Boche snipers. Then, too, if Fritz hears people passing through the trenches, he is liable to toss over a few grenades or "minnies" (minenwerefer shells).

* * *

You would be surprised to see how comfortable our rathole is! As I wrote you yesterday, it is below the crest on the hillside away from the Boche. He cannot hit it with a direct hit and it is splinter proof—that is, it is proof against shell fragments. About the only danger is that a heavy shell might come down and explode squarely on top of it, in which case, it would be demolished; or, a "big one" bursting in front of it might cave in the wall.

From the road you enter a narrow cut which becomes deeper till you reach the door, back about 20 feet from the road. Stepping in, you are in a room about 8 feet wide and 10 feet long. It is ceiled, top and sides with lumber and artistically paneled with waterproof paper. There is a window looking out through a cut like the cut leading to the door and there are curtains over the door and window. Not ornamental curtains but curtains to keep out gas and to prevent light from showing outside at night. There is a table, a washstand, shelves, clothes press, bed and chairs and a little woodburning stove. Over the table there is an electric drop light the current for which comes from our charged entanglement. Behind the planking of the walls and ceiling are heavy logs to hold and strengthen the walls and roof and all this was put in without disturbing the natural appearance of the hillside so a Boche plane, flying over us, cannot see that there is a regular village of dugouts. Regimental staff, or those of it who are up here at the forward PC live in the dugouts adjacent to the Colonel's and are connected by telephone with him, with La Croix aux Mines, with all parts of our line, and even with our division headquarters in Gerardmer.

* * *

Our fellows, like all American soldiers, seem to take a delight in mispronouncing the names of place over here or in giving them names of their own. They called Bligny "Bliny." Gerardmer was "Jeremiah" and now they call La Croix aux Mines, "Qualmine." Our forward supply dump, Haute-Goute, they call "Catgut," La Cude is "Cooty" and Violu is "Vuluu."

We are now, of course, in the "gas alert zones" and must expect a flock of gas shells or projectors at any moment. Masks are therefore worn in the "alert" position, up on the chest, flaps open and face pieces ready to slap on in an instant. We even sleep that way.

It is very late for the Colonel sits up till long past midnight waiting for something to happen. Early night and early morning seem to be particularly dangerous times. He is going to bed now—Good Night,

Your Soldier

SIX

THE LONGEST DAY, 1918

AFTER LESS THAN A WEEK ON THE FRONT-LINE VOSGES trenches in the friendly company of French troops, the back-and-forth nagging with the Germans escalated to battle. On June 17, the Lead Soldier wrote:

17 June 18
Dear Hugh,

One cannot foresee what may happen any minute in this business, after midnight, the Colonel put aside his maps, turned out the light, opened the door and window to air out the dugout and went out in front where he stood listening.

All was so quiet that it was hard to realize where we were—not a sound disturbed the stillness of the perfect night except the step of the gas alarm sentinel in front of headquarters and the hoot of an owl in the moonlit valley below us.

The rain had stopped, the night was soft and clear and the air was rich with the perfume of the moist firs. Above, the stars shown happily on the peaceful scene.

The Colonel came in apparently satisfied with the way things were going. He wound himself in his old plaid blanket and tumbled into bed probably to drop off to sleep thinking of you all at home.

An hour later, out of the stillness of the night, pandemonium broke loose—a storm of artillery fire, shell bursts and grenade detonations—the rasping roar of infantry fire—the whir of machine guns and, above all, the staccato tat-tat-tat of the automatics.

The old man bounced out of bed and hurried out onto the road in front of the dugout where he met the Adjutant—"What in thunder is it all about?" he asked but no one knew.

There was no firing in our subsector but there seemed to be a regular battle going on in the sectors to our right and left.

The Colonel and Adjutant came in, drew the curtains, lit the light and went to moving pins around on the map.

Meantime, the other staff officers had arrived and the runners and cycle-orderlies stood ready outside.

After a while, reports began to arrive from our CRs but nothing of moment was happening with them—all were alerted and ready to attack or repel an attack.

"Just waiting"—How much of war is described by those words "Just waiting"—How often that is the order in battle!

So, for over two hours the fight raged on both sides of us while we "just waited."

Then it all ceased almost as suddenly as it had started and the night was still again.

Reports came in through all liaison agents giving the details of what had happened. The Boche had made no real attack but he had subjected the sectors on our right and left to a very severe strafing, particularly those parts held by Americans.

Early this morning, the Colonel mounted Roan and went to visit our CRs and PAs. Everything was all right. Everywhere our men had sat quietly in readiness and behaved like veterans.

This afternoon, the Colonel drove down to Qualmine and Catgut to assure himself as to our supplies and ammunition for it is more than probable that the Boche's ignoring us last night means that he has something in store for us later.

Our headquarters and the headquarters of the French regiment, being here together, have combined their messes. They understand better than we how to get the produce of the country and we have the better commissary supplies. They have an artist of a cook and we too have a good one. Together they turn out dishes that would be a credit to Delmonico.

The mess room is a large dugout nicely furnished and prettily decorated by their French soldiers during their long occupation of this sector. Regiment after regiment has been here and each in turn has contributed to the equipment and furnishings till there is everything necessary for a really luxurious mess.

Breakfast, petit-dejeuner, is served in the dugouts for many of the officers are awake practically all night and are not required to be up early. Lunch, dejeuner, is more or less informal. But dinner is always a most elaborate ceremony.

The officers assemble outside the "mess hole" and wait for the two Colonels. When they arrive they salute each other with great formality, then shake hands. Then they return the salute of the other officers who are standing rigidly at salute and lead the way into the dining room. There, all stand at their seats till the Colonels have taken theirs, then all sit down but the mess officer who stands and reads the menu, always concluding with "Mes Colonels, messieurs, bon appetit."

The officers are seated alternating French and American, the Colonels sitting side by side.

In the center of the table there is always a bowl of flowers and a delicious dinner is served in courses.

It is altogether a most surprising affair to be happening within a kilometer of the Boche trenches.

Dinner ends by the French Colonel toasting the American regiment and our Colonel toasting the French regiment. The toasts are always drunk in "nuel" the poilu [friendly slang for French soldier] ration rum.

After last night's excitement and today's rushing around, I think the Colonel is pretty tired—I see him putting his gas mask on the table beside his bed—that means

Good Night,
Your Soldier

20 June 18
Dear Hugh,

Things have been livening up considerably since my last letter and our regiment is fast learning the game of trench warfare.

Of course, trench warfare is not what we are over here for but it is another step in our training for it not only accustoms the men to the sights and sounds of war but also it teaches them how to apply their instruction in the face of the enemy.

Heretofore, we have been playing a one-sided game—shooting at targets, bombing empty trenches, and bayoneting dummies. Now the targets have rifles, bombs come back from the trenches and the dummy uses his bayonet.

In training, when a patrol made a wrong move the instructor corrected it but now if it makes a mistake in "No Man's Land" some of its members die. Men are told to keep quiet and move cautiously in the training trenches—if they do not do it here a "minnie" will be their reproof.

But the greatest result of our work here is the whetting of the men's fighting edge—every little set-to with the Boche makes us the keener to go after him again.

The French division commander was here day before yesterday and had the Colonel in for a long conference.

He must have been satisfied with our work for he ordered the discontinuance of mixed sections of the line and turned over those parts of it entirely to us. Also, he withdrew the French battalion from the Grande Goutte Subsector on our right and assigned it to our regiment. The Colonel ordered up the First Battalion and put it here and brought the Second Battalion up to La Croix aux Mines, in support. So, now we have two battalions in the front lines.

* * *

For several days the Colonel and the Major and the French Colonel have been hatching out some scheme. They were out together all yesterday and again this morning fussing around in the forward trenches.

When the French General was here a day or so ago, he was very eager to get a Boche prisoner to get information from him and the Colonel suggested that a raid would be a good thing— not only to get a prisoner but to whet up our men. "My men are eager for the chance," he said—"They are begging to go over the top and it will 'pep' them up."

But you must understand that raid is by no means a simple thing to be entered upon without preparation. It requires days of careful preliminaries and it often costs thousands of dollars and a number of lives to get a prisoner.

Though the trenches are very close together, each has in front of it a strip of barbed wire entanglement and an electrified wire.

Behind the Boche obstacles are the trenches with men with rifles, machine guns, and grenades. In his support trenches, are more of them. Back of his front lines there are minnenwerfers and way back is the artillery with firing data all prepared for smothering any part of the front with gas or shells. Let Fritz catch a raid starting across No Man's Land. He will light it up with flares and star shells and literally tear it to pieces. Furthermore, if the raiders did get across, they would probably find the Boche front trenches deserted, their garrison having escaped through the Boyaux to the support line.

So, how can we get into his trench and, at the same time, prevent his getting out of it? One way is by calling the artillery to our aid. At the prescribed time, our artillery opens upon his batteries and pounds them so their efficiency is reduced. At the same time it drops a "box barrage" over the part of his line to be raided. A barrage is just a wall or curtain of fire—a line of bursting shells that no one can cross. If the wall is not only a line parallel to his trenches and behind them but also has sides running perpendicular and towards our trench; you see a part of his lines will be shut up in "box" which will not only keep its occupants in but also it will prevent aid reaching them.

At the same time some of our guns and trench mortars fire upon the enemy's wire entanglement and tear it to pieces. When the way is clear, our men go "over the top" preceded by a rolling barrage and dash into the Boche trenches with the bayonet.

The smoke and flying debris of the barrage conceal our men from view of the Boche artillery and he dares not fire on his trenches for fear of injuring his own men.

You can see how secretly all preparations must be made for, if the Boche has an inkling that a raid is coming over, he would drop his men back from the front lines and leave a clear field of fire for his artillery and machine guns which would burn up our raiders.

The Colonel is over in the artillery commander's dugout now and they are probably cooking up a party for Fritz. I'll bet my yellow plume it's a raid and I know where it is going to be, for, from where I sit, I can see the part of the map that the Colonel and the Major have been measuring and moving pins on for the past two days.

So long,
Your Soldier

In concept, the training program appears to have worked. An American regiment had first been integrated into a French division and then had taken over responsibility and, remarkably, even had a French battalion assigned to it. The test came soon.

World War II historians seem to have appropriated the title "The Longest Day" to celebrate D-Day, the June 6, 1944, landings of Americans on the beaches of Normandy. The day of the year with the most daylight, the longest day, is actually June 21, the summer solstice. That day in 1918 deserves praise in the annals of the 61st Infantry in the "quiet" sector of the Vosges. In her letter of June 21, Ida wrote, "The longest day of the year! I wonder how you have spent it." It would have given her no comfort to have known. On the following day, June 22, 1918, the Lead Soldier wrote:

June 22, 1918
Dear Hugh,
I was not far wrong in my guess—we raided the Boche last night and he raided us today. That is a habit of the Boche—he always returns exactly what he receives—I think he has an idea that he can bluff his enemy out of any wish to "start something" and of course he wants us to be quiet here so he can keep only a few troops here and have more for where he is now making his big push, north of Paris.

But our game is to nag him here and make him detach troops from his big fight to hold us. So, though we are not actually in the big battle, we feel that we are helping in it.

But I must tell you about our fights for we have had a full day of fighting and, after all, a little battle that one is in is more important to him than a big battle that he is not in and, for the men in the fight, a little battle may be a big one and he would be just as dead if killed in Violu yesterday as he would be if he were killed at the Marne in 1914. And a fight in which 10 of 100 men are killed may be as hot as the fight in which 10,000 of a 100,000 are killed.

Last night the Major and two of his company officers dined at our mess. They were the two officers chosen to lead the raid but no one except they, the Major, and the two Colonels knew it. Only those officers, the artillery commander and the adjutants knew even that there was to be a raid. The leaders had selected their men but had not notified them yet. After dinner they went over all the plans and they went off to assemble the raiding party.

The men were turned out quietly and "filtered" into the front line trench at the point from which the raid would "go over." There, everything was explained to them so that each man would know his part in the play. They were all enthusiastic and proud of being selected for there was not an officer, nor a man, in the regiment who would not have envied them had anything been known about it.

About 8 o'clock the Colonel assembled his staff and told them what was about to be pulled off. Arrangements were made to assure liaison during the fight and to notify company commanders in time for them to "alert" their companies just before "H" hour (the hour of attack) and hold them ready, under cover, to meet a possible counter attack.

* * *

Of course, the order for a raid has to be very precise and must cover every detail of the action of the raiding party, the artillery, the trench mortars, the supports and everything else that is or may be concerned. Roughly, our order prescribed that at H hour minus 15 minutes the raiding party should assemble in the front line trench between GC 5 and GC 6, La Cude. At H hour the artillery would open counter battery fire against the Boche batteries, drop a box over the portion of the Boche trenches to be raided and demolish the wire in front of them. At H plus 15 minutes, the raiders, preceded by a rolling barrage would go over the top, rush the Boche trenches, go through designated parts of it, bomb out the dugouts, take prisoners, and return before H plus 45 minutes when the barrage would be lifted. You see, then, that the artillery was to put its box around 3 sides of the Boche and our party was to follow the rolling barrage into the open side and have their own little fight down in the bottom of the box unmolested by anyone. It is like a terrier going into a badger hole and the badger has got to kill the dog or get caught and incidentally, the dog may have a rough half hour himself but he likes the sport.

Our men are keen sportsman and you would have thought, could you have seen the delight of the men chosen for this raiding party, that they were going on picnic instead of going on about the most hazardous undertaking that befalls the lot of soldier and more.

Everything worked out perfectly. The Boche apparently had no suspicion of what was going to happen and his lines and eyes were as quiet as a Quaker meeting.

At H hour minus 5 minutes the Colonels and their adjutants stood out in front of the dugouts waiting, the signal operators were at their instruments, cycle orderlies stood to wheel, chains of runner relays connected the PC, CRs, PAs and GCs.

As the luminous hand of the Colonel's watch reached 10 o'-clock—Bang Bow Whiz Boom Brrrr!—the ball had opened!—every gun of ours was tearing away at its assigned target—

"Voila" said the French Colonel. "As sudden as a summer shower!" replied our Colonel. "Fritz is getting his!" said our Adjutant. "Qu'il le recoive bien!" replied the French Adjutant.

The Colonel was right, it did fall like a summer shower but it was a thunder shower and I should not like to be caught in such a downpour of shells and such a hail of shrapnel balls.

"Tout va bien!" chuckled the French Colonel.

"Bully!" our Colonel replied.

Then they came into the dugout and stood pouring over the map trying, I suppose, to mentally follow what was happening at GC 5 and GC 6 and in the Boche trenches and to the wire between them—going over anxiously, no doubt, in their own minds all the plans and arrangements for this storm they had called down. If the plans were good and all contingencies were properly provided for, we should succeed. If mistakes or omissions existed, we should fail and our men would pay for the blunders with their lives.

These must have been anxious moments for the old man and though he was calm, and apparently, confident, his serious expression and the deepened lines of this face told of the tension he was under.

Soon the batteries replied to our fire and our guns redoubled their pounding. Our artillery had had the advantage of knowing in advance exactly what was to be done and they "got the drop" on Fritz who was evidently having trouble serving his guns, for, they did not slam back at us with their accustomed vigor and they were gradually pounded down to a weak and ineffective return fire.

Picture to yourself our men in GC 5 and 6 while this was going on! Crouching in a trench—faces hard and set—nerves tingling—hands gripping their rifles on which were fixed the gleaming thirsty bayonet—ready to spring like tigers at Fritz's throat—and the guns roared and the storm flew overhead while the watch ticked off: H plus 10, H plus 12, H plus 14, H plus 15.

"UP AND OVER MEN!—FOLLOW ME!"

"Brrrrrrng" goes the telephone on the table! "They're over, Sir," says the signal officer, replacing the receiver.

"God speed them," replied the Colonel, "The Boche can't stop them!" Then, a moment later, "Oh, I wish I were with them—it's so much easier than this!"

And then he went out in front of the dugout and stood, trying to hear, through the roar, some sound that might indicate the progress of the raiders. He could not hear and he could not see but, had he been able to, this is what he would have seen and heard:—"Up and over men! Follow me!" and two gallant young lieutenants sprang out of the trench, each followed by his party of 25 picked men. Each party in two lines of skirmishers, the second line about 10 yards behind the first. Half of the leading men were bombers and the others riflemen. In the second wave, there were fewer bombers.

The parties headed for opposite ends of the section of trench to be raided, hurried across No Man's Land, pushed through the wrecked entanglement, keeping as close as possible to the sides of the box.

At H plus 15 minutes when they jumped off, the guns that had been demolishing the wire dropped a barrage and it rolled over the Boche trench, forcing Fritz down into his dugouts as our men advanced. Then it crept on, halting behind the front line and establishing a wall there.

Following close behind the barrage, one of the raiding parties leaped into one end of the trench and the other party into the other end and then they began to work towards the middle, clearing the trench and bombing out the dugouts.

When they came to the entrance of a dugout they would call to Fritz to come out and if he did not come promptly, in went a grenade. If Fritz was met in the trench he had to fight or surrender, preferably the latter because we wanted live prisoners who could talk. So the fight in the trenches went on till the parties met at the middle and returned to our lines with 2 wounded Boche and a lot of equipment, insignia, papers and other stuff that might serve to give information.

One of the prisoners died soon after we got him in but the other is quite talkative and has let out some very important information.

We got out remarkably well—none killed and only 6 wounded so our first raid was a great success.

Of course it cost a pile of money but that does not count when a prisoner is needed.

This morning the Colonel went to La Cude to congratulate the men, then to Qualmine to visit the wounded who had been carried to our dressing station there. Then he went to Grande Goutte where the Boche were strafing our First Battalion. Fritz seemed to be in a bad humor over last night's performance or he was trying to draw our attention to another part of the line, preliminary to coming back at us here. It is a safe bet that when he makes his intentions obvious in one place he is getting ready to hit another.

Our entire line had been warned to look out for a return party from the Boche but the Colonel was particularly apprehensive about Violu Sud which is the most vulnerable part of our position. The shape of the hill there gives cover to an approach from the front and the Boche batteries dominate it. This morning a Boche plane was hovering over Voilu Sud till our anties drove it away.

Just before 2 o'clock this afternoon the Colonel put on his helmet, took his mask and started up there to GC 4 to look things over.

He was hardly out of the door when "Bang, Bang, Slam, Bow"—all the Boche batteries opened. The Major, who was with the Colonel, bounced onto his horse and lit out at the gallop for his CR and Colonel knocked over the chairs in his rush for the telephone.

There was no difficulty in finding out what was going on— the Boche had dropped a box over GC-4 where the Colonel and Major were headed for and if they had waited 10 minutes they would probably have caught them both.

For one solid hour they pounded away and their fire was heavier than ours last night for they have a superiority in artillery and they have gotten the drop on ours which they smothered badly.

They simply tore the road up between here and Voilu Sud— on one stretch of a 100 yards there were 56 direct hits. There was not a telephone wire left in the subsector, our wireless was shot away and the trees and rear of GC 4 were mowed down like hay. The valley below, where the "overs" landed looked as though it were on fire. We were getting what we gave the Boche last night and it was a perfect storm of steel and lead.

At 3 o'clock p.m. the Boche came over—a splendid raid of a hundred stosstruppen (shock troops) especially selected and trained for this kind of work.

The preparation for their assault had been fine and they bounced into our trenches as we had into theirs. Our front line had been badly mauled by the artillery—every man in GC 4 had been killed or wounded but, when the barrage had rolled past them the men in GC3 spread out and covered GC 4. They were outnumbered by the Boche and were fighting a losing fight when a platoon of the company support rushed forward and threw themselves upon the Boche with the bayonet and ousted him from the trench.

Fritz took no prisoners back with him when he started for his lines on the run but he left us one prisoner and he left more dead in the trenches he raided than we had men there defending them.

His stosstruppen can think it all out now and figure that when they shock American troops they must shock hard.

Later the Colonel went up to GC 4 and what a wreck it was! The dugouts were caved in, the trenches broken down and, in places, quite filled in. For 200 yards along the front of our trench the wire had simply disappeared—there was not a vestige of wire left nor the sign of a post that had supported it. There was not a tree, a bush, a shrub, nor a blade of grass between the Boche wire and our trench and the ground looked as though it had been plowed by a drunken farmer with wild horses.

That is what modern artillery can do! Are you surprised that we have to live like gophers. I could write you a lot more about this raid but don't you think this is enough?

Good Night,

Your Soldier

The efforts and bravery of the 61st were recognized by French general T. Dauvin, who wrote a commendation to the regiment, which translated reads:

To the P.C.

Anould Sector

June 23,1918

General Dauvin, Commandant P.I.

21st Infantry Division

to MONSIEUR the Commanding Colonel 61st R.I.U.S.

My Dear Colonel,

I have learned of the good conduct of the American Garrisons of C.R. VIOLU and LA CUDE during the night of June 21 and the evening of June 22.

I address my compliments to you, to your Officers and to the valliant soldiers of your Regiment; particularly to the troop that last night occupied G.C. 4 Of P.A. Violu Sud for their courageous attitude.

I am happy to have, in you, comrades in combat, who from the first, give proof of their solidarity and bravery.

Receive, my dear Colonel, as testimony of my satisfaction, the expression of my best and very devoted feelings.

T. Dauvin

The Lead Soldier should have elaborated more. In the later award of the French *Croix de Guerre* with Army Palm to the Colonel, Order No. 22.243 of the French Army, translated, lauded:

> Colonel Hugh D. Wise, Commander, American 61st Infantry Regiment. Brilliant Officer who maintained very high morale of his troops by his beautiful courage and his great cold bloodedness in the moment of danger.
>
> This is particularly noted June 21 and 22, 1918 where by his skillful positioning and his energetic attitude he dealt a serious blow to the enemy's hand.

Of course, June 21 and 22 were not without deaths. They happen in uncelebrated battles, as well as in the notorious ones. The Lead Soldier wrote:

24 June 18
Dear Hugh,

Today has been the quiet after the storm—maybe that both sides are tired after the last few days or perhaps the big guns have sore throats from so much barking.

The French Division Commander, our Division Commander, and the Corps Commander have been here today and we have received a handsome letter from the French General commending the regiment.

This afternoon we buried our dead. On account of Boche shellfire we could not have many men assembled—only two from each company. It was a small little ceremony but an impressive one, there on the hillside behind the trenches.

After the chaplain had read the burial service he asked the Colonel to speak to the men and he said "Men, this is no time for eulogies—we have just started upon the stern work we were sent over here to do—we are burying our first men killed in action.

"Here, in these blood-stained blankets are our comrades who have given their lives for our country. These blankets are soaked with good American blood that runs in the veins of nearly 4000 more of us in this regiment who stand ready, if need be, to follow the example of these brave fellows. We must not mourn these men—there must be no mourning for men who fought like heroes and died as martyrs in this, God's Cause.

"It matters not that they are gone. So much as how they went.

"We shall miss them in our bivouacs and we shall regret their absence from our firing line but we are proud of them—'Three cheers for them!'"

And it was cheers, not sobs, that went up from the little cemetery on the hillside.

Camp Frame,
April 1918.

Dear Hugh -

Certainly, I never
expected to go to a real war
and your hand must have
been the hand of fate when
you took me from the box and
gave me to the Colonel saying: -
"Here, Daddy, take this
little soldier with you to
write me what is happening."

Opening of Col. Hugh D. Wise's first letter to his son, Hugh, Jr., in the voice of the Little Lead Soldier, dated April 1918: "Certainly, I never expected to go to a real war and your hand must have been the hand of fate when you took me from the box and gave me to the Colonel saying: 'Here, Daddy, take this little soldier with you to write me what is happening.'" (*Hugh D. Wise, III*)

Hugh D. Wise as a young officer.
(*Hugh D. Wise, III*)

Ida Hungerford, Hugh D. Wise's future wife, as a debutante.
(*Hugh D. Wise, III*)

The Wise sons in September 1918. From left to
right, John, Richard, and Hugh, Jr.
(*Hugh D. Wise, III*)

The troop transport *Pocahontas* carried Col. Wise and the rest of the 61st Infantry Regiment to Brest, France, in April 1918. (*Naval Historical Center*)

Col. Hugh D. Wise in France, 1918. (*Hugh D. Wise, III*)

The ruins of the town of Malancourt in the Argonne sector after the battle (*Library of Congress*)

The ruins of the town of Montsec in the St. Mihiel sector after the battle (*Library of Congress*)

ARGONNE SECTOR.

TOWN OF MONTSEC, IN THE ST. MIHIEL SALIENT.

An infantry attack in the woods at Argonne. (*Library of Congress*)

Romagne Cemetery, France, where more than 23,000 American soldiers killed in combat were interred, including those from St. Mihiel and the Argonne. (*Library of Congress*)

SEVEN

IGNORED BY BLACK JACK

ENERAL PERSHING WAS HIGHLY CRITICAL OF THE
training given by the French to the American troops
stationed in the quiet sectors such as the Vosges. Pershing wrote: "Training in the quiet sectors in association with
French divisions, upon which the French laid so much stress,
had proved disappointing during the past months, as their units
coming out of the battle line worn and weary, failed to set an
example of the aggressiveness which we were trying to inculcate
in our men. . . . After considerable experience, it was the inevitable conclusion that, except for the details of trench warfare,
training under the French or British was of little value."[1]

During the days of the fighting that led to the regimental
commendation given to the 61st Infantry and the Croix de
Guerre awarded to its commanding officer, Black Jack had spent
his time looking over other American troops in the Vosges. Ignoring the contribution being made by the 5th Division and its
61st Infantry, Pershing noted in his diary of June 22 only that
the training of the 32nd Division was promising.[2]

On July 2, the 61st was relieved from its station on the front by Annamites (Indo-Chinese, probably ancestors of the Viet Cong, later determined and successful adversaries to both the French and Americans). In 1918, they were led by French officers. The 61st was sent to the villages of Arche and Archettes, two small towns across the Moselle River from each other and a short distance from Gérardmer to the southwest, to rest and clean up.

On July 4, Ida and the boys were in Watertown staying with relatives, but not with her father, who was recovering from what appeared to be a stroke and was not well enough to stand the commotion of the uprooted family. In her letter of that day, she wrote that she had not received any letters from her husband since that of June 10, shortly after he had arrived somewhere that he could not disclose. That somewhere was Gérardmer, and the time was just before he went to the front-line trenches. On July 4, Ida still did not know that her husband had been in combat, or even whether he was dead or alive. On that same day, the Lead Soldier described the new surroundings:

July 4

The Colonel came on here to our new area yesterday in his car so we beat the troops here—they have to travel very cautiously, and usually at night, till they get out of proximity of the enemy.

Today all the regiment has arrived and we are located, headquarters and part of the regiment in Archette and the remainder across the river in Arche.

If you think that a rest area is a place to loll around and take life easy, you are very much mistaken. A soldier said "It is a place they work you so hard and where the 'change from the lines' is so much worse than the trenches that you want to go back."

Our training schedule here calls for work from 7 o'clock a.m. til 4 o'clock p.m. seven days a week, with one hour out for lunch.

The first day is given the men to clean themselves and their equipment and, of course, their billets and then starts the training. This period of training will differ materially from those we have had for we will train mainly for open warfare which everyone believes will start very soon. It will therefore be largely maneuvers of the regiment, brigade and division.

If you will find Epinal on your map you will see the place which is only 5 miles from us. This is the famous Moselle Valley and it is perfectly beautiful though entirely different from the Vosges where we were.

It is a lovely gently rolling country with fine pastures, rich cultivated fields and luxuriant gardens. The towns and villages are almost undamaged by the war which has affected them only in an occasional bombing from the Boche avions.

Today, the regiment is going through the "Cootie Wagon"— that's what the soldiers call the "Mobile Disinfector and Delouser."

Lice, called "cooties," were a terrible problem. They bit. That led to scratching and the spread of bacterial infections. However, the Lead Soldier, having no blood for their feast turned philosophical:

That sounds pretty bad, doesn't it? But it is true, just the same. You would not know much about this war if you did not know something of our little companion, the "Cootie."

The French say he is of Boche origin and the Boche blame the French for him but, whatever be his nationality, all trenches and dugouts are full of cooties and they become attached to Americans.

Whenever troops come out of the trenches they have to be freed of cooties so the Cootie Wagon comes. That is a huge boiler and steam sterilizer on wheels. The men are given a good hot bath and while they are taking that their clothing is put through the sterilizer.

There have been millions of poor little cooties cooked to death here today, but "C'est la guerre." And this is the cootie's fate in it. If there were no war there would be no Cootie Wagon and while a peasant might occasionally catch a cootie and murder him, there would be no such wholesale slaughter as at present—just so with me—in peacetime, a criminal sometimes kills another man but thousands are not murdered in a day. But, in war, men's lives and cooties' lives are taken by wholesale.

Our Constitution states that life, liberty and the pursuit of happiness are inalienable rights of men. The British Magna Carta and the laws of France reiterate practically the same principle. These rights are, in fact, the basis of modern civilization and it was because the Boche attempted to curtail them that the peoples of the civilized world brought up the developments of scientific warfare to maintain these rights.

The cootie claims only these same rights and yet these same people bring up this scientific insecticide to exterminate him.

Seems to me that you flesh and blood men are not always consistent—you are fighting the Boche because he denied you the same rights that you kill the cooties for claiming. You censor the Boche for using his might to make his right and you use your might to deny the cootie his rights. You claim liberty to go about the world in pursuit of happiness but you deny the poor little cootie his liberty of crawling around on your backs in pursuit of his happiness.

It seems to be just a question of size and force and, if the Allies are strong enough, they will maintain their rights over the Boche as they deny his rights to the cootie. So, after all, might is right!

But we should not forget that size is only relative and that, absolutely, both men and cooties are very small.

To a cootie a man's back is as big as is a town to the man, how small the town is on the earth! How small the earth is in the solar system! How insignificant the solar system is in the universe! So, running backwards down the scale, universe, solar system, earth, man, cootie—man is so infinitesimal that the cootie can be no less so and, if the little man has rights why is not the little cootie the same?

If a cootie is simply a parasite on the little man, why is the man not simply a parasite on the little earth?

* * *

This is "the day we celebrate"—the 142nd anniversary of our independence for which we are still fighting today. But the people we fought against 142 years ago are our allies and our best friends today. These are the same people as we are in blood, language, and tradition and they stand shoulder to shoulder with us in this struggle for the rights of mankind.

We have had no celebrations today—not even music, for our band did not arrive until late. Is it not funny that the first day in a fortnight that we have not had fireworks should be today, the 4th of July.

Good Night,
Your Soldier

Those who opposed the rights of mankind were the Germans and those aligned with them. The German might was invested in its sovereign, Kaiser Wilhelm II, a man maimed from birth with a withered arm, the result of a difficult entry to the outside world. He turned out to be the last ruling member of the Hohenzollern dynasty, which had ruled Prussia under various titles since 1525. There was a parliament, the Reichstag, made up of men elected by eligible male voters at least twenty-five years old. It had limited powers, but an important one was the right to control military spending through issuance of war credits. The Reichstag was presided over by a chancellor appointed by the kaiser.

Wilhelm had complete control over foreign affairs and the military. He was an autocratic, xenophobic man, convinced that Germans were entitled to more than they had been allotted by the rest of the world. To the kaiser, the Germans were the best, and yet were not accorded that position in the European hierarchy. He was also an unrelenting optimist and cheerleader who believed in the superiority of Prussian military force.

In 1916, the kaiser had appointed the sixty-six-year-old aristocratic Paul von Hindenberg as chief of staff of the military. He and his chief deputy Erich Ludendorff had received credit for the spectacular turnaround German victory over the Russians at the Battle of Tannenberg in East Prussia in the early days of the war. Ludendorff joined Hindenberg in Berlin in the same nominal capacity, but exercised actual control over the German military effort, at times relegating Hindenberg and the kaiser to figureheads.

Ludendorff was a man of ideas and aggression. In his glory days, he epitomized the arrogance of German militarism. To American cartoonists and George Creel's propagandist machine, he could not have been better. He

> personified the restless energy and surging power of the German Empire; he also personified its ugliness, its crudity and its fatal unwisdom. Under his *pickelhaube*, (the German military helmet which had a spike at its top) bright, keen, protuberant eyes stared out of a suety, pudgy face ornamented by a straight nose, a bristling moustache, a pursed mouth, and sometimes an eyeglass. His head was round, hair cut short and bristly, his brow high and broad; a beefy neck bulged into the uniform collar with the gold and carmine general officer's collar badges. Ludendorff was tall and straight, but his sword-belt sagged slightly round and beneath a heavy stomach. His manner, his entire personality expressed restless ambition and impatience, an enormous appetite for action.[3]

He was a perfect villain.

On June 9, while the 61st Infantry was still in training at Gérardmer, Ludendorff attacked the Allies at Montdidier-Noyon on the river Matz.[4] The German troops were repelled by the reinvigorated French and the attack fizzled on the 14th.[5] Ludendorff and the other brass did some thinking. The Germans no longer had numerical superiority and their numbers were being even more reduced by a virulent influenza that, although it struck all forces, had greater effect on the Germans because of their dwindling manpower. But, to give in would not do. On July 3, the Kaiser, Reichstag representatives, and the High Command met and agreed that the minimum and necessary terms for concluding the war were the annexation of Luxembourg and retention of the iron and coal fields of French Lorraine,[6] close to where the 61st Infantry was stationed.

Once again they concluded that to accomplish their goals, the war had to be won by military might, right now. On July 13, the Reichstag authorized new war credits in order to get the job done. To achieve that goal, Ludendorff was faced with the options of attacking the British positions in the Flanders area of Belgium, which would lead to the English Channel ports, or pushing to Paris. He selected the more showy option of capturing the French capital. July 15 was the day selected to begin the offensive.[7]

The Allies also conferred. On June 1, 1918, they agreed that for each of the months of June and July, 250,000 Americans would be transported by British and American ships. Priority was to be given to combatants, but some desperately needed railroad workers also would be sent.[8] The brass gave scant consideration to the miserable conditions that would be created by cramming that many people onto the limited shipping available.[9] While American troops were pouring into France, the question was how wide the spigot could be opened.

On June 23, General Pershing hosted a conference at the American headquarters at Chaumont, attended by Premier Clémenceau, Marshal Foch, and others. It was agreed that the U.S. Department of War would be asked for enough additional divisions to reach a total of eighty by April and one hundred by July 1919.[10] At that conference, Clémenceau, who had met with Pershing before Foch arrived, expressed support for the early formation of a separate American army. When the premier departed, Foch, however, reiterated to Pershing his desire to place American troops under French command.[11] Once again, Pershing resisted, and, there being no resolution, once again the can was kicked farther down the road.

The Allies got word that the Germans were planning a big push to begin on July 15. Among many other preparations, the French troops, to whom the 61st Infantry had been attached, were withdrawn to go to the "big show," but apparently, General Pershing did not think the 5th Division was ready. By then, the 61st had been moved to the trenches around Moyenmoutier, a short distance to the north of St. Dié. The Lead Soldier wrote:

Moyenmoutier
14 July 18
Dear Hugh,

My last letter was written on our Independence Day, this is the great French day—the anniversary of the fall of the Bastille.

We have moved again. Our training period at Arche was cut short by the urgent need of troops in the lines. The British and French are making a tremendous drive to the west of us so we were hurried here to relieve a French regiment and let them go in.

It was disappointing to us that we should relieve other troops to go into the "big show" instead of going in ourselves. The Colonel hated to lose the training that we were to have had but the men were glad enough to get away from the "rest area." One soldier said that with another week of rest he would die of exhaustion.

Find Epinal on your map again. Then look almost northeast of that about 30 miles and you will see St. Dié. We are in the Vosges again, about 10 miles from St. Dié.

We move this time in a new way.—the Third Battalion made a "camion trek" (troop truck) all the way from Arche. The Second Battalion camioned halfway and marched the other half. The remainder of the regiment marched all the way.

The regiment therefore came into the sector gradually each battalion relieving a French battalion which then marched out. The change was thus made without a jar or a break in the security of the lines.

This is the Rabadeau Sector of the St. Dié front. The right half of our regimental lines is called the La Forain Subsector and the left, Mère Henry (Mother Henry) after the mountain of that name which is the key point of the position.

When the Third Battalion arrived yesterday it went into the Mère Henry position and today the Second Battalion took over La Forain. The First Battalion is coming into the reserve position at Etival, about two miles in the rear, behind the Meurthe River.

Two machine companies have been permanently attached to the regiment so we now have a machine gun company with each battalion.

In this sector, we shall have no French troops. We are now considered competent to "go it alone."

The lines are well fortified and heavily wired as they were at Brial and are divided into GCs, PAs, as they were there.

Fritz seems to be the same old Fritz and his game would be not to cause trouble or distractions here. It has recently been a rather quiet sector but the Colonel has orders to stir it up a bit more so Fritz cannot detach troops from here to go to the big fight.

Our PC is in a magnificent chateau which is all ours. The proprietor has gone to quieter parts leaving only his caretakers here.

Driving down the main street of the pretty town one is surprised at seeing how little it has been damaged by Boche shells although their lines are less than about 3 or 4 kilometers from here.

The reason is this—there has been an unwritten understanding that the Boche would not shoot up Moyenmoutier if the French did not shoot up Senones, a town about the same distance behind the Boche lines. The Boche have some workshops in Senones which evidently they do not want destroyed and, naturally, the French did not wish to injure the French town nor kill the French women and children there. This understanding, which we are ordered to respect, brings about some queer conditions. Our batteries shell the Boche lines and all the villages near them and their batteries do the same to us. But Senones and Moyenmoutier are spared. Their planes come over and bomb everywhere but Moyenmoutier and ours go over and bomb everything but Senones. It is quite a nuisance to have to plan all our operations so as not to hurt Senones and it must be equally annoying to them to have to respect Moyenmoutier.

When one reaches the middle of the town you come to a high stone wall, by the iron gates of which stand two smart looking sentinels. Driving in and around a circular drive through a pretty yard, full of flowers and ornamental shrubbery, you stop under the porte-cochere of the chateau.

An orderly opens the big carved door and you step into a handsome hallway at the end of which are winding stairs leading up to the next floor. On the left is what used to be the reception room, upholstered in yellow silk. It is now the personnel officer's office. Back of this is the sergeant major's office. It used to be the "salon" and its handsome furniture has been stored and replaced by the plain tables, desks and chairs of the regimental clerks.

Through a plate glass door from the salon, you enter the magnificent library where the Colonel and adjutant have their office.

Across the hall is the immense dining room with its handsome big table, leather chairs and walls decorated with deer and boar heads. The table is big enough for the headquarters mess and we have the use of the silver, china, glass and utensils and of the kitchen and pantry with their paraphernalia.

Upstairs are rooms for the Colonel, Lieutenant Colonel and several members of the staff—all handsomely furnished and decorated.

On the third floor are rooms for the orderlies, cycle orderlies and chauffeurs and in the cellar are bombproofs all connected up by wire with the forward and rear positions and with our division headquarters, as are also the Colonel's office and the adjutant's.

In the yard is a garage and a splendid stable.

Now is not this "War Deluxe" and it all less than two miles from the Boche guns!

The French Colonel remained in command today and will remain here until the transfer of the sector is complete. He is a big fine fellow and we shall hate to see him go.

He and the Colonel have been out all around the lines and, in one place, they had a very close call from a minnie but they both came in laughing about it.

Good Night,
Your Soldier

It was not War Deluxe at the big show. When their great offensive began on July 15, the Germans threw fifty-two divisions at the French positions between Reims and Soissons. They intended to storm on to Paris and end the war, relegating the Vosges and everywhere else to irrelevance. Thus began the Second Battle of the Marne. The kaiser was there to watch and exult when Ludendorff triumphed, as expected.[12] The Germans crossed the river Marne, but met stiff resistance from the French troops and five attached American divisions.[13]

On July 17, the German offensive stalled. The next day, twenty French divisions, to which the American 1st and 2nd were attached, began a massive counterattack that pushed the Germans back, and the kaiser went home. There were heavy American casualties and lavish praise was showered on both the American divisions that had held in defense and those that had attacked.

By many accounts, the German defeat at the Second Battle of the Marne was the end of any chance that Germany could win the war. There were not enough recruits to replace those soldiers who had fallen. Not only were the American numbers overwhelming, the Allies were effectively using tanks, as never before. According to historian Correlli Barnett, Ludendorff's personality "disintegrated." Barnett also wrote: "From this day forward danger and desperation never left Ludendorff. Yet the brutality and weight of the French counter-stroke, coming only three days after the dismal failure of the last of so many supreme German efforts, seemed to smash the governor that controlled Ludendorff's restive energy, so that the powerful machine began now to race itself to pieces."[14]

Nonetheless, the war went on. From the forgotten shadows of the Vosges, the Lead Soldier recounted the activities of the 61st:

Moyenmoutier
23 July 18
Dear Hugh,

We have been holding this sector a week now. A command passed a week ago this morning when Colonel Blondel, with his Adjutant, facing our Colonel and Adjutant said: "Mon Colonel, je vous rende le commandement." "I receive it," replied our Colonel. Both saluted and this was then an American sector. We have here our regiment, six batteries (3 heavies and 3 light), a battalion of engineers, and some detachments of special troops.

Before Colonel Blondel left, the Colonel had been all over the sector with him and since then the old man has devoted nearly all of his time to studying it. All day he is out somewhere on the lines and until late in the night he is working over the maps.

Here in his office he has maps on the walls that show every detail and all of our positions and the Boche positions. On these are colored pins and bits of paper which are moved about to follow the changes of the troops. One map is kept posted to show all the information our patrols have learned, another gives the firing data on different points called sensitive points. These are the places in the Boche position that may be "worthy targets"—that is worth shooting at. Sometime every day the Colonel, the artillery commander, the intelligence officers and several others have a great pow wow over these maps and spend a lot of time shifting and moving pins around over them. It seems to be a regular game of theirs.

Then, too, they study the sector from the observatories. There are several of these. Way up on the peak of Mère Henry is our observatory, "Jean-Pierre," from which one looks over nearly all the sector and that is where our command post would probably be in the event of an offensive. Near it are two others, the French "Army Observatory" and "Le Nid d'Aigle" [Eagle's Nest] the artillery observatory. Le Nid d'Aigle is especially interesting because it is blasted and hewn in the solid rock face of the cliff overhanging the valley far below.

All these observatories are equipped with splendid telescopes, binoculars, range finders and other instruments and trained men in them watch, day and night, everything that moves in the Boche lines or behind them.

Besides these there are several smaller observatories and OPs (Observation Posts), such as "Mère Henry," "Salome," and "Korman." These are under the subsector commanders and give closer though more restricted views of certain points.

The observatories and OPs are all connected by telegraph, telephone, visual signal and runner relays with company, battalion and regimental PCs. You might pass right in front of one of them without suspecting it was there, so perfectly are they concealed—only narrow slits open to the front and they are cleverly camouflaged with brush or grass.

* * *

The telephone is rarely used except for conversation that would not be of use to the enemy or in great emergency when we disregard the danger of the Boche hearing.

Now how do you suppose he can get our messages from our wires that do not connect with his instruments?—just as we get his! By the "listening in apparatus." This is a wonderful electrical apparatus which is so sensitive that an electrical current passing over wire several miles away may cause a current to be produced in it. If the Boche Colonel talks over his telephone to his front line, we hear every word he says—it's just plain eavesdropping, isn't it? Our position here is not so well under cover as that at Brial and many of the roads would be in plain view of the Boche were it not for the camouflage. One can get to Mère Henry without being seen but he has to be mighty careful going to La Forain and in the valley between them he has to travel through the trenches and covered ways for, if Fritz sees anything move out there he slathers the valley with machine guns and sprinkles it with shrapnel.

The camouflage does not hide the dust that rises behind an automobile so, unless it is a damp day, that is a dangerous way to travel. If you go on horseback and they open on you then you wish for the speed of the car. If you walk, you are too slow so, whatever you do will probably be wrong.

At Brial we could take forward supplies by day but here this has to be done at night. Even then the Boche tries to catch the supply carts on the way up so we dare not have a regular time for it. Sometimes we make noises on the roads and behind the lines similar to the noise of distributing rations to draw his fire and when he is through with his shelling then we quietly distribute them.

***

Ever since we came here we have been active and very aggressive with our reconnaissance. Not a night passes that we do not have out four or five patrols and two or three times a week we make some kind of a little raid on some part of the Boche line.

The Colonel has published an order forbidding the use of the term "No Man's Land." He said there is no such thing as "No Man's Land"—that is ours and we are going on it when we please and the Boche must be kept off of it.

We have been working very hard to get a prisoner to confirm or disprove a report that the Boche have been reinforced by some Austrians but Fritz is very leery about risking himself outside of his wire and that is very thick.

Some way, he has learned about us. The very first day we were in the sector, they called from the trenches—calling the regiment by name and telling us they heard we were coming—asking how we liked Brial and how were our little Chinese brothers.

What they were alluding to was that a day or two after we left Brial, the Boche raided the Annamites whom they handled rather roughly, capturing several of them.

We are having all kinds of fun worrying Fritz with our Stokes mortars and our 37 mm guns. The officers commanding these platoons are very energetic and very game and the Colonel has directed them to continually harass the Boche. Of course, they are delighted and never lose an opportunity.

The little 37's are extremely accurate, very light and easily moved and concealed. They fire a wicked little high explosive cell which is death and destruction to a machine gun nest or to a "pill box." Their purpose is to knock out machine guns and woe betides the nest that the 37's locate.

A day or so ago, the Colonel was going along the road back to the crest of Mère Henry. He met the 37 Lieutenant with the crew pulling up the guns. "Where are you going with your toys?" asked the old man. "We've located a pill box sir and we're going to smash it."

"Will you let me have a shot if I go along with you?" asked the Colonel. "Delighted, Sir, Come along" replied the Lieutenant and the crew chuckled with pleasure at having the old man join in their sport.

A few yards further up the road, the crew lifted a gun and cradle off the axel and carried it up to the top of a little knoll. There they set it up behind some bushes. Then, with pocket knives, they cautiously cut a hole through the branches keeping hid all the time from Fritz.

Looking through the hole you can see, about 300 yards away, a thing that looked like a big concrete pill box with a square hole in it through which poked the muzzle of a machine gun. The pill box was about 6 feet in diameter and was probably about the same height though only about 2 feet of it showed above the parapet of the trench in which it stood. With the glasses could be seen a couple of Boche gunners looking through the window beside their gun. We had to be very careful that they did not see us and turn loose the leaden stream at us from that gun before we tossed them our present. Furthermore, we realized that if we missed with our shot, they would mow down our brushes before we could fire another. Meantime, the lieutenant was calculating his firing data and whispering it to the Colonel who was sitting on the trail adjusting the sights. Presently, he looked up, smiling at the Lieutenant, and whispering: "There you are!—That's got 'em!—Get the men under cover !"

The men slid down behind the crest and the lieutenant focused his field glasses on the pill box. "Ready?" whispered the Colonel—"Ready, Sir"—The Colonel's finger closed on the trigger and Bang—Wh-s-s-bow!—There was no more gun muzzle in the hole and no Boche looking out but a stream of yellow blue smoke curled out of it.

The men darted to the gun and rushed it back—Bounced it on its axel and raced back down the road before the Boche artillery should have time to turn on them.

He did cut loose at the place we had been and I'm afraid he ruined our friendly bushes but we were all gone.

Up the road a way, the Lieutenant said: "I guess we got that pill box!" "Rather," replied the Colonel, "And it must have been a little crowded for the gunners in there with a half a pound of TNT. Thank you for your entertainment, Lieutenant, where are you going now?" "Over towards GC 4. There's another over there that we want today—Won't you come with us?" "Thank you no" replied the Colonel—"I wish I had the time—It's a great sport—Good Luck!" In the evening the Lieutenant reported that they got the second pill box.

Good Night,
Your Soldier

While her husband was doing she not knew what or where, because the last letter she had received from him had been dated June 22, the day following the longest day, Ida and the boys bounced between the houses of family and friends in her hometown of Watertown. I am unable to find Ida's letters from July 8 to July 21 and so I do not know her reaction to Hugh being on the front and engaging in combat. She did read encouraging news of the Allies progress in France, but the newspaper reports revealed nothing about the 5th Division and its 61st Infantry. So, she wondered and wrote lonesome letters every night.

EIGHT

STIR IT UP

O N JULY 24, 1918, WHILE IN THE CELEBRATORY MOOD because of the victories that repulsed the Germans during the Second Battle of the Marne, British general Haig, Marshal Foch, French general Pétain, and Pershing met at Foch's headquarters. Flush with enthusiasm, Foch presented a memorandum for offensive action.[1] The formation of an American army was again discussed and agreed to, although Pershing pointed out that the Americans still needed to rely on French artillery and the French agreed to supply that artillery when needed. At last, on that day, Pershing issued an order establishing the First American Army to be effective August 10.[2] That army, which was to consist of the divisions that had been fighting on the Marne, was to be stationed in the Marne sector. It did not include the 5th Division and its 61st Infantry.

Although ignored by Black Jack, the 61st was at its post and doing its job, inglorious, dangerous, and, at times deadly, a sideshow to the impending big show. From July 26 to August 4, the Lead Soldier wrote in part:

26 July 18

Dear Hugh,

We were told "to stir the sector up a bit." I don't know just how much a "bit" is but, evidently, the Colonel takes it to be a liberal measure for he keeps things boiling and never lets them settle.

The Boche absolutely will not come out of his trenches and he is so securely wired that we cannot get in at him. Our reconnoitering patrols, everywhere, come up against his wire and when they are discovered trying to cut through it—sizz!—out goes a star shell and by its light, Fritz opens with machine guns and artillery and drives in our patrols. In the same way, he stopped all of our stronger efforts to get at him and about all we have accomplished is the keeping of him in a state of nervous anxiety.

If we could use our artillery for demolishing the wire and putting a box over Fritz we could raise him but there is such a demand for ammunition over with the big push that we are restricted in the use of artillery ammunition here and use it only for necessary counter battery fire or an emergency. Even this necessitates quite an expenditure of ammunition where the Boche is very generous with the shells he sends us.

* * *

Since we cannot use our artillery to cut wire for us and to cover a big raid as at Voilu, we have to resort to all sorts of schemes to get openings in it.

In a number of places, we have cut small openings by determined men, camouflaged with grass and leaves, who crawl out at night and snipping the wire with wire cutters. Another way is by the "Bengalore torpedos." These are simply sections of tin gutter pipe filled with high explosive. These are pushed out under the Boche wire and set off by an electronic detonator or by a friction fuse. One would blow a gap about 20 feet wide. It makes a terrific explosion and, of course, Fritz, expecting a raid to rush right through the gap, opens up with everything he can reach it with.

Sometime a gap that has been quietly cut is repaired with string so the Boche will not know that there is a gap there and we may use it for our patrols. Many other gaps are left to entice the Boche repair parties into our ambushes.

We now have a dozen or more openings through the Boche wire and keep on making more. He evidently thinks this is preparatory to some important operation and he is correspondingly nervous. Any noise in the vicinity of one of these openings will set him off—bang! And shooting so our men have no end of fun playing tricks on him. They have strings tied to the Boche wire so they can shake it. They throw tin cans out into a gap or talk through a megaphone so the sound of their voices will seem to come from there. A few days ago, our men rigged up some dummies and fixed them so that, by pulling ropes, the dummies would be made to slide forward like men crawling across No Man's Land. That brought an awful fusillade.

The Colonel permits and encourages all this because it worries Fritz and keeps our men interested and amused.

* * *

While we are so busy on the ground, there is a lot of activity in the air. Boche reconnoitering planes are frequently over us and ours are over the Boche. Occasionally, a bombing plane comes over and drops its "eggs" and ours bomb them. But little damage is done this way because the "antis" keep the avions so high that they can bomb with no accuracy. About the greatest danger to the troops, as well as to the native population, from the aircraft, is the danger from fallen shell fragments and shrapnel balls fired by our "antis." Whenever a Boche avion comes over, a signal is given and all soldiers and civilians take to cover.

You would see in every town near the front, signs on certain houses—"Abri," which means that these houses have cellars prepared for protection against shelling. Others are "abri contra gaz," or gas proof cellars.

Most of the air activity here is simply reconnaissance and photographing. Most of the bombing is done in the rear areas. They have bombed our railhead at Raon-L'Étape several times lately and our bombing planes have been over after their rail heads.

Four days ago, 19 of our planes went over, headed north on a bombing trip. When they go on these expeditions they fly in a "V" formation like wild geese. They were very successful on this trip and almost destroyed an important Boche rail head.

The most interesting thing we see here in the air are the frequent combats between our planes and the Boche planes. A day or so ago we watched one of these fights from our office windows. Our man was going out to photograph a Boche trench we were going to raid. A Boche plane dashed over the mountains and headed him off. They flew at each other like two hawks, circling, rising and diving—each trying for an advantageous position over the other, and, whenever he got a favorable opportunity, bursting off his machine gun. They continued circling and climbing as they fought until they were finally lost to sight above a cloud.

That night, our man came in and brought the photograph. He told the Colonel that he had gotten the better of the Boche but had to give up the pursuit because the Boche flew back over his lines and went so low that he could not be followed on account of the Boche archies.

28 July 18
Dear Hugh,

Today is Sunday but you would not know it here by any difference from another day. The war does not rest on Sunday nor do we nor the Boche let up a bit in the fighting. In fact, this morning started as most mornings do with a lively artillery duel. It seems as though the big guns, having slept part of the night, wake up fresh and happy and, like the birds, want to greet the golden sunshine with their songs.

So, every morning, while the little birds in the trees in the chateau yard are singing of life and happiness; the big guns about them are hissing death and misery.

From the window of the Colonel's room, we can see the position of one of our batteries, about a half a mile across the grassy slope.

This morning while the Colonel stood in the window, shaving, he was watching the Boche shells bursting around that battery and our guns replying to them. I thought what a queer performance that was. But it really is not unusual for he does it quite often—he has to shave and if he waited until there was no firing in this sector he would wear a long beard which he does not permit in the regiment. Having given the artillery all the orders he has to give, it is not his business to serve the guns nor is it his policy to interfere in the work of the officers and gunners. He is about as safe in the window as he would be anywhere else except in the cellar and the window is more interesting.

All this sort of thing—the irregular life—uncertainties, strain—excitement is just a part of the soldier's business and is to be expected so, I cannot feel sorry for them as I do for the civilians in the towns. For four long years they have been suffering hunger and deprivation and have lacked the comforts and conveniences which, before the war, they regarded as necessities.

There are here only men too old to go to war or men home from the front, crippled; women too old to work in munitions works or hospitals; and children—pathetic little things whose fathers and brothers are at the front or who have died there.

It would make your heart ache to see these old white-haired men toiling in their little gardens to eke out an existence for their families and these bent old women slaving over wash tubs when age entitles them to be sitting leisurely on their doorsteps enjoying this soft air and bright sunshine. But here they are willingly replacing at domestic labors the younger generation which is fighting or working for France. They offer no complaint of hardship nor do they bewail their losses—they simply struggle on and pray only for victory for their country. If one wants to see the spirit of France, he does not need to go to the trenches for here it is in the simple courageous people.

Our big, strong, lusty boys are kind and considerate of these unfortunate people who are their defenders and protectors since the departure of their own troops from this sector, and, so on their part, the people are most grateful and appreciative. So a bond of sympathy has developed which makes our relations with the population easy and pleasant. They open their little homes and give our men a fireside to sit by and our men, in their spare time, carry wood and water for the old women or help the old men in their gardens.

Since we have been here, there has not been a single case of misconduct towards the native·population nor a complaint from it against our men.

But the most pitiful of all are the children! They are not sad nor unhappy for they are children and they do not realize what they lack nor do they appreciate what a strange life they are leading. They have been underfed for four years and have forgotten or never knew what it was to be otherwise.

The constant plowing up of the meadows about the town by the Boche shells forbids these playgrounds to them and they must remain close to the "abris" into which they may at any moment have to dive. To them the roar of battle is little more than the noise of the streets is to you. They see columns of troops marching up to the lines and trains of ambulances returning but there is nothing extraordinary in that—they have seen it happening for years. The "avions signal" and the "gas alert" are part of their routine life. They go trooping off to school with their books and their gas masks and, to them, one is as natural as the other.

Poor little things! They are living in war, some of them were born in war, most of them know no other condition but war. Their homes are practically on the front lines and the very atmosphere they breathe is tainted with the smoke of battle. Yet they play as other children do, unmindful of the horrors that surround them and unobserving of the pinched faces and pale cheeks that war starvation has caused them.

The Colonel often stops to watch their games and I know he is longing to do something for them and thanking God that his boys are safe and sound in a quiet peaceful home.

Almost every day the people send flowers to the Colonel. He, of course, knows that this is not a personal tribute to him but an expression of grateful appreciation by the people to their American protectors for the Colonel commands that cocky line which stands between them and the Hun savages on the other side of Mère Henry.

But there is one little personal bunch of flowers in an empty 75 millimeter cartridge case on the Colonel's desk and he loves them. They are brought by Suzanne, a little girl who lives next door with her old grandmother and her crippled brother. Her father is a prisoner in Germany, two brothers were killed at the Marne, and, a year ago, her mother was killed at her front door by a Boche shell. She is a great pet of the Colonel's and whenever he goes to St. Dié or Raon-L'Étape he is quite sure to return with candy or treats for Suzanne.

There was a high mass in the church here today as it was an official celebration of some sort, the Colonel and the staff attended.

While the services were going on, two Boche planes came over and our anties opened. For half an hour above the chants of the priest, we could hear the boom of the guns and the whirr of machine guns. In the midst of the services, an orderly hurried in with a message that required the Colonel to leave this form of religious duty and go out to another service to God, fighting the Boche.

And so it is here with everything. The war is ever present. Battle and the routine of life are inextricably mixed. Birds sing while guns roar. Children play in the valley while men fight on the hill. Prayers go up from the congregation while shrapnel balls ring on the cathedral roof.

We can have no band concerts here because the music and the gathering of a crowd would probably tempt the Boche to shell the town and kill non-combatants. Furthermore, the band is split up doing duty as stretcher bearers on the line. They have done splendid service as they did in the Brial sector.

One time, at Brial, the Colonel got the band together and had a concert right up behind the front lines in pure defiance of the Boche and also to tempt him to start something and we were all alerted and ready for it. But Fritz evidently suspected a trick and kept perfectly quiet. But that concert must have been objectionable to him for the band played "Watch on the Rhine" and Deutchland Uber Alles with horrible dischords. By the way, do you know what the tune of Deutchland Uber Alles is? It is the old church hymn Glorious Words of Thee are Spoken.

* * *

Later

I wish you could have been with us this afternoon for you would have seen a fine show and you would not have been in much danger. Just as I guessed, something was going to happen when we left the office—our artillery gave those machine gun nests opposite our right an awful strafing but where do you suppose we watched it from ?—up a tree!—inside the tree! Looking out through a knothole 40 feet above the ground like a squirrel. That may sound foolish but it is the truth. It was a camouflaged tree.

Our trenches out on the right center of the La Forain line are in the edge of the woods. The lines are close together but the thick underbrush makes it difficult to see the Boche lines without getting up above the ground. Whenever sentinels tried to get a look out up a tree the Boche would drive them down and he was vigilant in hunting for them in the trees.

From his constant shelling of the woods, many trees have been cut off or felled so that all along our forward trenches there are many tall trunks standing. One of the biggest of these was a tall fir, cut off about 40 feet above the ground, leaving only the bare trunk standing. When the French were here they decided to make this tree a lookout. They sent for the "camouflage corps." It came and took measures and photographs of the cut off tree, went back and made one of iron exactly like it and, one night, brought it here and laid it on the ground beside the real one. Then, on a dark night, they lowered down the real tree and stood up in its place the iron and no one can tell the difference for they were exactly alike in size, shape and color. Even the knotholes in the splintered top of the real tree were perfectly reproduced in the iron one.

At the foot of the iron tree, you go down into a hole under the trunk and then climb up through it on hand and foot holds to near the top. There you find a little saddle like a bicycle saddle and, sitting there, your eye is opposite a fake knothole through which you look out over the Boche trenches, right where we had our party today.

Usually the Boche makes trouble for us in going to that part of the line for the road is exposed to his review a great part of the way. The camouflage is in poor condition and, in some places, it is shot entirely away so one has to run the gauntlet. Today, however, Fritz was as quiet as a lamb and though our party took up the run across the danger stretches, as usual, he did not fire a shot at us which was most unusual.

At the woods, our party dismounted and crept cautiously through to the further edge. There the Colonel went up the tree I described and the Lieutenant Colonel up another. They took their seats about a minute before the performance started and they sat there comfortably and watched it through, in regular first row orchestra seats about 200 yards from the center of the stage where the Boche were playing (Hide and Seek with our shells).

One of the first shells landed squarely on top of the pill box and smashed it to smithereens and many others ripped and tore in and among the Boche trenches. It must have been a perfect inferno for the Boche that were caught in that part of the line.

29 July 18

Dear Hugh,

I told you that the Boche would come back at us for the straf-ing we gave him yesterday!—There was no doubt in predicting that for Fritz is very punctilious about returning our compli-ments. And how the old man found out exactly when and where the Boche were going to shoot us up, I do not know. I think it must come through our "listing in service" for this morning it picked up a Boche cipher message which we partially decoded and, during the day, several fragments of conversations were quite confirmatory that Fritz was up to something.

This afternoon the observatory at Korman reported that they could hear the Boche moving some guns or minenwerfers and Jean-Pierre reported several suspicious things.

How they figured it all out, I do not know but I do know that at about 3:30 p.m. (15 hours 30 minutes) the Colonel sent a mounted officer to the CO at La Forain to inform him that his line where it crosses the Moyenmoutier–Senones Road would be shelled at 16 hours 30 minutes (4:30 p.m.) and to di-rect him to draw back the men from the GCs to avoid the shelling and to hold them ready to advance as soon as the shelling ceased. Meantime the artillery commander was directed to lay his guns on the "Hesse Trench" in front of the threatened point. Promptly at 4:30 p.m., exactly as anticipated, the Boche guns opened and for 30 minutes they viciously shelled our empty front trenches while the men, drawn back into the support trenches, laughed at the waste of ammunition.

Then they quit and our men re-occupied the trenches and, during the night, repaired them. It was a fine object lesson to us to be careful about talking over the telephone and a good ex-ample of how little scraps of apparently unimportant observa-tion may be pieced together to give information of inestiminable importance.

Old foxy Quiller Boche does not often make mistakes as he did today but his indiscretion cost him the success of his plan, whatever it was. He burned thousands of dollars worth of ammunition and the only hurts he caused were some blistered hands from trench repairing and some aching sides from laughing at him.

30 July 18

That particular neck of the woods down in the valley where the Moyenmoutier–Senones Road crosses the trenches seems scheduled for the interesting scenes of the last few days and this afternoon the Stokes mortars had their turn.

Salome and Korman have both been recording lately that some work was going on in a little copse just back of the Boche front line. Wheelbarrows loaded with sacks of sand and concrete have been going in there and working parties go in and out every day. The Colonel has had it carefully watched, not only to learn what they are up to but also to decide upon the best time and method to go after them. They seem to be building pill boxes behind the trees which they would cut down after their pill boxes were complete leaving them dominating several of our GC's.

Beyond all doubt we did know that in that little copse large working parties were busily engaged and that, whatever they were doing, it was not for our health nor comfort.

As soon as he had definitely located the place where they were working and learned the time when they were thickest in there, the old man sent for the Stokes mortar platoon commander—"Stokes" he said, "you know where the Boche is working, out there in the copse in the Senon road?" "Yes sir, I do." "Well, don't you think you could touch 'em up a little?" "I can indeed!" the lieutenant fairly shouted with joy, "My men are itching for the chance—we can burn 'em up." "All right," said the Colonel in as matter of fact a way as though he had been telling Stokes to police his billets, "Clean'em up. I think 4 p.m. will be a good time. Send 'em about half and half—gas and H.E.'s (high explosive shells)."

Stokes had been longing for this chance for days—he bounced out of the PC and fairly ran to his platoon to give glad tidings to his men. In an incredibly short time, his platoon was setting up the guns and laying up piles of shells beside them in an old quarry behind our lines opposite the copse.

Long before the appointed hour, they were ready and impatiently waiting. On the tick of 4 p.m.—"BLUIE"! went all the mortars in unison and then a steady roar as they each sent 15 shells a minute over into that little half-acre of woods where 200 unsuspecting Boche had been at work. The quarry hole belched up a perfect stream of tumbling shells which, glistening in the sunlight, formed a shining arc, like a rainbow with one foot at the guns and the other in the copse from which drifted the nasty yellow mist of gas.

Five hundred shells, half of them gas shells, in that little copse, in 3 minutes, must have made it a deadly place to be in and we feel pretty sure that the building enterprise of that locality suffered a serious set back.

Our plan was to do our work quick and clear out before the Boche artillery could get busy. That is what the Stokes did— three minutes of rapid fire and they piled out of their hole and scampered for safer parts. Hardly were they out when the Boche guns simply slathered their quarry and its vicinity and, again, Fritz made a "water haul."

The Colonel watched the show from the Korman OP. He brought Stokes back to the mess to dinner. They were both in high spirits over their success. The Colonel told the mess that it "was simply beautiful." Beauty, of course depends largely upon the viewpoint—I do not believe it was beautiful for the Boche in those woods.

Good Night,
Your Soldier

31 July 18

Dear Hugh,

There has been no more work in the copse and Korman reports that during the night the Boche were busy carrying out a number of dead and wounded from there.

Last night we blew several gaps in the Boche wire and also we pulled off a little raid up on Mère Henry. We cannot get much result there, however, because the Boche have that part of the line so perfectly covered by their artillery and minenwerfers and machine guns.

The top of the hill is a saddle. One knoll, the pommel, being ours and the other knoll, the cantel, is the Boche's. The seat, between them, is no man's land. This has been an awfully bloody place for the French and Boche have fought back and forth over it for four years. It is estimated that the French have had nearly 10,000 casualties here and the Boche have probably as many. The French took the Boche knoll several times but had to give it up every time because it is swept by the fire of the Boche artillery on Ortomont, a high hill in its rear.

The whole saddle is completely cleared of trees by shell fire and the ground is all ploughed and torn up.

The lines up there are less than fifty meters apart so sniping, bombing, and rifle grenading are incessant. All day and, at night, it is lighted by rockets, flares, and star shells. It is always Fourth of July on Mère Henry!

Our observation post is dug into the ground and covered with steel plate and earth. Through a narrow slit in one of the plates, we can look right down into Senones where the Boche colonel's PC is—not a thousand yards away. Often, we see the Boche colonel and his staff officers. Were it not for that order forbidding firing into Senones we might easily "pot" them—it is a great temptation to our men.

He is a big fat fellow with a yellow mustache and a straight back to his head—he looks just like pictures of Boche.

We did bag one of this staff officers a day or so ago—he was in the habit of riding out to the edge of town where, dismounting, he would enter a communication trench. He was most regular in making this trip and our look outs had studied his comings and goings until they knew his ways.

On the day we got him, he and another officer rode out and then dismounted and entered the trench at the usual place, where we could not shoot at them. But, a little way from the edge of town, they came up and walked along the parapet, evidently studying the ground and apparently forgetting that they were outside of the immunity area. Meantime, one of our best sharpshooters was following them with his sights and when Fritz got where he wanted him "Crack," he dropped him, a great shot at 1200 yards! We lost one of our best young officers today on Mère Henry.

The Boche have up there several big concrete machine gun nests. They are so strongly built that our light artillery cannot smash them and they are so close to our lines that we dare not use our heavies on them. This morning our light artillery and trench mortars made it so hot in the Boche nests that the gunners fell back. The lieutenant saw a chance and, as soon as our shelling ceased; he and one of his men crawled forward, carrying a charge of high explosive, to blow up a concrete nest that had been annoying his company. They reached it and were placing the charge when they were discovered and showered with grenades. They got back, both wounded, but the Lieutenant died.

It was a daring enterprise undertaken on the Lieutenant's own initiative. Had it succeeded it would have relieved us of one of our greatest annoyances in that part of the line and the Lieutenant would have received a cross—a bronze cross. Now, poor boy! He gets a wooden cross but he was a hero just the same.

4 August 18

For the four days that this letter has been laid aside, things have been stewing along. I do not try to tell you in my letters all that is happening here—I hardly know it myself—it is just typical trench warfare kept seething all the time and frequent little minor operations. Shelling, bombing and sniping goes on all day and every night there are patrols, little raids or "bengalore" parties. It might be a nervous strain were we not all so accustomed to it that it seems quite normal.

What I've written you are accounts of some of the different kinds of entertainments so you may have an idea of what trench warfare is like. There have been many more like those I have written of and others that were combination of them. For example, the Stokes mortars and the 37's often work together or with the machine guns or all of them may join in with the artillery and with the infantry too.

Here is a stunt we pulled off last night:—Information has for some days convinced us that the Boche trenches opposite the Lamdebahay section of the Mère Henry sector were quite strongly held but at one place, opposite our GC-40, the Boche line runs out to a point which we figured we might be able to break off. But all along there the Boche had dozens of machine guns and his wire was unusually thick.

For days we have been scouting and patrolling and have even had aerial photographs made to learn what was in front of us there.

It was evident that we could not have any success unless the attention of the Boche was diverted to some other point so we began being particularly annoying to his Hesse and Wurtemburg trenches down in the valley to the right of GC-40. There where we had so many doings a week ago and Fritz seems still rather nervous about that vicinity.

In the meantime our men were sneaking out every night and cutting wire in front of GC-40 and tying it up with string so the cuts would not show.

Our machine guns were placed so as to concentrate their fire on certain Boche machine guns from which we anticipated special trouble and the 37's took up concealed positions, each being laid for a particular pill box selected as its victim.

And now for the big joke! The Stokeses were set up in a ravine and laid so their shells would fall in a line in front of the

Hesse trench. By each gun were placed 4 piles of ammunition, each pile with heavier charges than the preceding one so, as the gunners ran through their ammunition, the range increased and the barrage of bursting shells would creep forward like a regular artillery rolling barrage.

After dinner, the Colonel mounted Roan and, with the signal officer and several orderlies, rode off up to the Lamdebahay to see the fun.

At H-1, 9 p.m., a party of scouts went out from GC-40 and cautiously opened the path that had been cut through our wire. A few minutes later, a squad of engineers went out and quietly pushed bengalores under the Boche wire. They were followed by a raiding party of forty picked men armed with shotguns, pistols and trench knives. Their clothing was covered over with leaves and branches of fir, their faces were blackened, to prevent their showing plainly in the glow of star-shells, and they looked more like they were going to a carnival than to a hand to hand combat in the enemies' trenches.

They crept out quietly through our wire and lay about 20 yards from the Boche wire where the bengalores were to open the gap. At H hour, 10 p.m. a rocket went up near the PC Lamdebahay. Immediately the Stokes dropped their barrage in front of the Hesse trench, the 37's cut loose at their pill boxes and the machine guns commenced rasping away to keep the Boche gunners from their guns.

A moment later the hill shook and the landscape was lighted by the explosion of the bengalores.

The raiders sprang forward and rushed the Boche trench but that was not the part we feared—it was the returning that we feared for them—they had their machine guns held down but suppose their artillery should cut loose on No Man's Land in front of GC-40? That is what it was the Stokeses game to prevent and their ruse worked perfectly—the Boche artillery seeing the barrage creeping towards the Hesse trench supposed that there was where we were raiding. They promptly opened a counter fire down there and simply tore up the valley with shells while our party scampered back into GC-40. We had two men wounded and killed several Boche but we got no prisoners. When the explosion occurred the Boche in the front line rushed back through the boyaux to their support trenches which were so lighted by flares and star-shells that our men could not follow into them.

The whole thing on our side was over in about 30 minutes but there had been such a racket that Fritz evidently thought we were making a real attack and until long after midnight he was shooting and shelling our line.

Soon after the daylight the Colonel came riding into the chateau yard, well enough pleased with the way things had worked except mad and disgusted at getting no live prisoners— "We had a bully sail," he said to the adjutant, "but we didn't get a whale."

Good Night,
Your Soldier

After a delay of over two weeks, the Lead Soldier again wrote:

20 August 18
Dear Hugh,

It has been a long time since I wrote to you—not because there was not lots going on here but because most of the shows have been more or less like what I have told you.

Since I wrote, however, there have been a couple of fracases hereabouts that were more important than the ordinary ones.

August 17, the brigade on our right took the town of La Frappelle and straightened out a Boche salient there which was menacing our division's position.

We did not become involved but while the fight was going on, we were alerted and stood ready to resist any diversion the Boche might make or to make one ourselves if called upon.

The H-hour was 3:00 a.m. and maybe they did not kick up a racket. They got the town that morning but the fight kept up in a desultory way all day, the Boche continued to shell them in the captured position and to gas them heavily.

A day or so after this, the Boche made an attack on our lines down in that same old troubled valley. It opened with a shelling of the Poterosse section of the La Forain sector and, while the shelling was in progress, they tried to amass troops in the trenches opposite there. We found out what they were up to and our artillery spoiled their game. The fight spread all along our line and was quite lively for several hours but the Boche had no success anywhere and we think we handled him pretty roughly.

Today we pulled off a matinee performance which, for cool daring, beats anything done here before.

Before daylight this morning, a young officer and four of his men, armed with pistols and trench knives, sneaked out through our wire and the Boche wire, got across the Boche front trenches, and hid in a boyau in rear of them till daylight. They had passed back through the boyau and, getting out of it, worked their way through the brush back close to the sub-sector PC. There they made important observations and started back. On the return trip they met a party of four Boche and in a hand-to-hand fight, killed them all. The noise of the fight brought out Boche trench patrols. Our men heard one of these coming through the boyau and hid around a turn. When the Boche patrol reached their hiding place, they sprang upon the Boche and wiped them out. Then, climbing out of the trenches, our men ran the gauntlet for our lines.

The officer and two men got back with valuable information and the Colonel has recommended them for crosses.

We are soon to be relieved here and to go we know not where but probably into the big show.

We are to be relieved by a French regiment which will divide a sector with a new American regiment for its instruction.

* * *

Goodnight,
Your Soldier

The Lead Soldier had described the typical trench warfare that General Pershing decried. To the general, fighting from trenches was the cause of the four-year stalemate. He did not want his troops to be trained by the French for such engagement, but the 61st Infantry had needed that training. That is what its soldiers had been doing for the previous two months.

When the Colonel's war days were over in the Vosges, as they were on August 20, he may have wondered, and others certainly have, what he and his men had accomplished. As seen in the Lead Soldier's letters, the soldiers were playing games, with death to the loser. It is easy to imagine similar thoughts on the other side of the barbed wire.

The raids, counter-raids, traps, and counter-traps were not intended to produce territorial gain and none resulted. The deaths to the losers in those games would not be remembered as having occurred in some great heroic event. Getting the enemy to waste ammunition was a goal. So was diverting enemy personnel from other fronts. As an active and imaginative man and a career soldier, the Colonel wanted more than games of no ultimate importance.

So far the Colonel had avoided death. There was another peril that the Colonel had averted so far. Never mentioned by the Lead Soldier, another killer, the influenza epidemic, was exacting an enormous toll.[3] One-third of all Americans who died in the war were killed by the flu. Worldwide 21,640,000 would die before it subsided in October 1918. The ships carrying troops across the seas were incubators, but President Wilson would not halt the transports. If he did, the Germans might conclude that the steady stream of Americans might cease.

The army's chief of staff, General Peyton March, declared, "Every such soldier who has died (from influenza on a troop transport) has just as surely played his part as his comrade who has died in France."[4] The general could have rationalized the death of a Vosges combatant the same way. He had died for a greater good, even though he did not personally participate in the endeavor.

The Colonel's career had almost been derailed by the yellow fever that he had contracted in Cuba, which came close to preventing him from going to the Philippines. Luckily, he had avoided the flu. The Colonel was now out of the trenches in the Vosges and on the path to action. Hopefully, he would be promoted and fulfill his quest to emulate the legacy of his father and grandfather. Now, he had the luck and opportunity to create his own legacy.

NINE

LAME

IN LATE AUGUST 1918 THE COLONEL WROTE TO HIS WIFE:

27 Aug. 18

My own Darling Ida—

You will now understand why, in my last few letters, I told you I was so busy—I could not tell you in them that we were being relieved in the sector and it is no small job to change troops in the front lines facing the enemy. However made the change successfully and, on Friday night, (Today is Tuesday) we started our march back to here.

The first night was a very hard one for the men were tired and soft from a month in the trenches and we had to take precautions more than usual against avions which had been rather active for the past few nights.

We reached billets about 3:00 a.m. in a rather poor locality though I had a comfortable enough place. Saturday we marched at 2:00 p.m. and had a better march arriving in very good billets about sunset. Here I had a luxurious place with every comfort including that unusual luxury in France—a bath tub.

We did not march till 5:00 p.m. the next day so the men were well rested and in better marching form and it was a splendid march to this place though the Boche avions circled over us once and drove us to the cover of some woods though they did not get any bombs in among us. They did, however, bomb some neighboring towns. They are irritating things—especially at night when it is practically impossible to get back at them.

On this march I rode my little thoroughbred mare "Violu" (named after the fight in which the regiment was commended). She is a fine little mare—pretty and good-mannered and not so big and rough as old "Roan" who has now passed to my orderly, Sgt. Mullins. On the march, I followed my regular custom of riding a while at the head of the regiment, then stopping and letting the column pass and then walking rapidly up to the head again—to see that the gait and formation were right. Time and again, on these trips, the men of some company would cheer me and it made me very happy.

I was never more impressed with the size of a regiment than on this march—Once, from the tail of the column which was winding down a hill, I could see the head going up the hill across the valley nearly three miles away—We now have two extra machine gun companies with us—Three miles of troops, guns and machine guns. And I kept thinking, "They are all mine."

You can imagine how proud I was of commanding this splendid force returning from a month of handsome service in the line—and nothing but praise of their gallantry had been their lot in reports.

But what I enjoyed most was ambling along through the moonlit fields and woody-adorned forests dreaming of you. As the sunset and its golden beams swept past, I sent you, by them, the usual messages.

We reached here at 3:00 a.m.—the men singing and, when I halted to let them pass to billets, each company cheered me as it swung by. Isn't it enough to make a man ambitious and to make him pray every night to be fit to lead these splendid men.

I love every one of them. There is no other duty like duty with troops.

I did not get up till 8:30 a.m. when faithful Riley brought me my breakfast. A little later, Blanks came in saying: "Colonel, this was here when we arrived but I thought it best not to give it to you till you had some sleep."

He handed me an order to appear before a medical board. Of course, I have feared this for five years but I was not at all suspicious of it now. In fact I felt that I was going better on my bad leg. I have not missed a day of duty in France—have not omitted a duty—have been in every trench of every position occupied by my regiment repeatedly—have marched horseback with my regiment regularly instead of going ahead in a car as some other colonels do. Both the Division and Brigade Comdrs. have spoken to me of the amount of traveling around my command I do and have complimented me on it and I had begun to believe I would get by, when Bang. What I have feared hit me—I have feared that piece of paper a thousand times more than I ever feared Boche bullets. I went to see the Brigade and the Division Commanders and found that they were powerless now in the matter.

The Brigade Commander was required to report any physical defect in his colonels and a special order from A.E.F. directed him to carefully observe them.

I can blame him only for not speaking of it but he said he wanted to spare me all possible worry—Perhaps it was right for had I known about it earlier, I should have had a miserable march instead of a pleasant one.

I was ordered to report to the 7th Corps Hqrs. Where I went yesterday and today I received an order to report to the Replacement Division for examination, but the Div. Commander has authorized me to go to A.E.F. Hqrs. and see whether McA— can help me in any way.

The regimental surgeon's report which accompanies me states that he has watched me in and out of the trenches for six months and that I was perfectly able to do a colonel's duty.

I have just signed the order turning over the regiment (Thank God, in the rest camp—not on the lines). My bags are packed and tomorrow morning I go to face what I have so long dreaded.

Last night, I sent a motor-cycle messenger for Barney (brother-in-law) who is at S-D—about 40 miles from here. Barney came about midnight. Of course there was nothing he could do but I wanted to talk with someone and I knew I could get good advice from him as he has had experience with such boards.

He thinks I will not be "canned" but put on some staff duty but even that is an awful thought for I lose any place in the line and I am afraid, if I am found unfit for line duty, my chances of a star will be gone. Barney says not and he is sympathetic and reassuring—I hope he is right. At any rate he was thoroughly sincere in his concern for me and I am glad I sent for him.

Oh, Ida, if you knew how I have dreaded this day which I felt would surely come. How I have schemed and toiled and struggled to keep it off and to be as capable as other men. How sweet the commendations I have received over here have been—not because they were flattering to any vanity but because they helped camouflage this physical defect.

I have taken many million of steps over here and every one of them has been an effort and a discomfort but I can take them joyously if they keep me at the head of my regiment and in line for promotion.

God knows I have done my best and I hoped I deserved better than a disability board.

Sweetheart, I do not want to become a "has been" right when success seemed in my reach. I do not want my boys to see me stop when others go on climbing up the ladder. And nothing I can do seems to offer the chance—this leg seems to have lamed my career as well as my body.

I want to have a name my boys may be proud of as my father and grandfather did. There is comfort in the consciousness that I have done my best but my best is very disappointing if they stop me now. But I will fight for it and try to keep out of the "cannery."

I am game and will accept what they throw at me and try to be as calm as I have been when the Boche were throwing their cross, annoying missiles.

9:00 p.m.

I stopped for dinner and after that the officers of the regiment came down of their own accord to say goodbye. I almost broke down for their expressions of regret at my leaving were so manifestly sincere and so flattering. I had no idea how fond they were of me—I knew the men were and I thought the officers liked me, as a rule, but they showed affection and loyalty far beyond my due.

The band came of its own accord and played a programme of the pieces the leader knew were my favorites—you know them too.

Then, after it was all over, a number of them came up to my room and sat a long while and asked if I could take them with me if I went on some other duty.

When they left—I broke down and cried it out like a baby.

This has been an harassing letter, hasn't it Sweetheart. I really wish I had not promised to write you so fully—But you ought to know and you shall. Don't worry—Before you get this it will all be settled and even though they shelve me now, I can be happy—they can take the object of my ambition away but they cannot take away the love of the dearest one in the world and if you and my boys love me and have faith in me the rest does not matter.

It will shorten the "night of waiting" and we will start our trip down the "Long, Long Trail" so much the sooner—Perhaps not as satisfied with what I have accomplished but just as happy in our love—

Goodnight, Sweetheart—I love you

Hugh

28 Aug. 18

My own Darling Ida—

I, never in all my life, felt more lonely than I do now sitting here alone in my room in the Hotel de France in the city where the A.E.F. Hqrs. are.

Of course, I have a lot of friends and acquaintances here and I might look them up but I do not want to see them for they would naturally take a friendly interest in why I am here and I do not want the matter known nor discussed. I want the whole question and examination stopped and the less said of it the less difficult it will be. But I do long for you tonight for if you could put your arms around me and tell me it would all come right I would believe it and feel easy—Oh, Sweetheart you are such a comfort in trouble and I have grown to be so dependent upon you.

When it is merely a question of bullets and shells I am never worried but when it comes to the question of this physical defect of mine, I am terrified for I know my left leg is an infernally bum one and, if they find it out, I am a "goner."

Last night I wrote you about being ordered for examination. I also told you that I got permission to come here and present my case before going to the board at B—.

This morning at 6:00 a.m. I took my little locker and dispatch case in my car and started out.

Blanks, who is a splendid fellow and a lovable man, wanted to come with me but, on account of an extremely important movement, it would have been impossible and I would not permit his even requesting it. When he told me goodbye he broke down and cried and I came near to it. I have grown to love the boy and trust him implicitly and I told him that, whatever the result of this incident, I could never come back to the regiment for it would be folly to again expose myself to the observation of the Brigade and Division Commanders who had taken the present action.

The officers and men at regimental headquarters were there to see me start and their affectionate regret touched me to the quick. How I managed to keep back tears and smile as I waved "Bonne Chance," I do not understand.

Reilly, who has taken such perfect care of me wanted to go with me. Sgt. Mullins, my orderly, who has ridden many miles with me all over our sector asked me to get him transferred to where I was going and when we reached this place Hall, my chauffeur, asked if I could not do the same for him. Isn't it gratifying and flattering to hear these men, so loyal and so affectionate. I do not know why it is for I certainly do not pamper them and, all my service, I have been known as a man who requires the limit of effort—yet my men always want to follow me—I think they know I love them and realize that I try to be just and fair.

Lt. Brone, the French officer who has been with me for four months, and of whom I am very fond, appeared at breakfast and announced that he would like to go to C— with me and that he needed no permission but mine. He said he was anxious to visit Ch— [Chaumont, A.E.F. headquarters] on business so I let him come. On the way, I accused him of faking and asked why he came. He replied that Blanks could not come and that he, Brone, could not bear to think of my going off alone on such an unhappy trip.

I was delighted to have him for he is a fine fellow—more like a Scotchman than a Frenchman and it made the 90 mile ride more pleasant. The day was perfect and the roads fine so we reached here about 10:00 a.m.

Depositing the luggage at the hotel, we drove to the Hqrs. where I made an appointment with McA.— and then Brone and I went to lunch. At 2:00 p.m. we drove back to Hqrs. where I had a talk with McA. and showed him my orders and the surgeon's report.

He was very friendly and interested. I told him I had been as bad and worse than now for at least three years and had not failed in any duty as a result of it and that it seemed pretty rotten that the carrying out of a rule should serve me this way—He asked the solution and I told him to revoke the order of the division sending me before the board, based on what I might not be able to do and give me a chance till I failed to meet some requirement none of which I had yet failed in.

I said too that when both physical strength and gait failed to carry me I shall be willing to quit for when I cannot play the game to glean the cards and I have too much patriotism to let selfish ambition make me an encumbrance on the campaign. He said, "You have been commended in action in the line—why don't you ask for duty where your leg can not be so taxed"—I wanted to be with the troops but, I would do anything except Q.M. rather than be "canned."

He called in Elting who handles that part of it and told him to see what could be done and tomorrow he is to tell me my fate.

Half a loaf is better than no bread and the funny thing is that my half loaf is what many men call cake. It seems the sane thing to do is to take a staff job if I can get it and forget my love of the line—It is not my wish but it seems my only hope and tonight I find myself hoping for what three days ago I would have spurned—"C'est la guerre."

Brone and I returned to the hotel and then he started back hoping to reach there by 8:00 p.m.

I hated to have him leave for I am fond of him—He has been my confidential man, who with Blanks, by my side in all of our little fracases at Violu and San Die and Moyenmoutier and Rabideau etc.—It seemed like casting off the howser and loosing the last tie that bound me to the regiment that I built.

I gulped hard as I said "Good bye Brone—Bonne Chance."

He and Mrs. Brone are coming over to visit us after the war. Of course, I do not know her but she must be all right to be that fellow's wife.

It makes it somewhat easier to leave the regiment because so many changes have taken place. There is not a major with it whom we started with. Many of the captains are new. Transfers and casualties have upset the lieutenant roster etc. etc.

Yet it is the 61st—my regiment and I love it.

It is eleven P.M., Sweetheart. I did not go to bed till midnight last night and was up at 5:00 a.m. this morning.

Yet my sleep is sweeter after I have poured out my heart and mind to you. Your photograph is looking at me on my table as it does in chateaux and dugouts—Whatever else changes you are the same—

My own darling, loyal, sympathetic wife—

Goodnight—I love you—

Hugh

31 Aug. 18

My own Darling Ida—

My last letter to you was Aug. 28 at — where I was sitting alone in the Hotel de France wondering what the next day would bring forth. The next morning I went up to A.E.F. Hqrs. where I found they had been over my papers and issued an order for me to return and take command of my regiment.

I offered no suggestion—Just asked for a car—got it—loaded in my plunder and by noon was speeding back—On the way I passed Bain Les Bains, one of the great resorts but now quite closed up and dead though still beautiful. The roads were full of American troops—All this part of France is and one sees more Americans than Frenchmen everywhere.

Arriving at R—, I reported to the Corps Comdr. And sped on to A—, reporting to the Divn. Comdr., but stopping en route at R-a-B (Raon-Aux-Bois) where I had left my regiment the day before. In the meantime, a hurry order had arrived and the regiment was gone—Had left in trucks that day for this place, about 30 miles away. But the supply company was just leaving it, of course, marched, so I put my roll and chest into one of the wagons and went on to A—. Here I sent the car back to C— and started on in a motorcycle side-car.

I hoped to reach here by daylight, but soon before dark a blowout stopped us. This, fortunately happened near a village where the cyclist and I got some eggs and bread. It was past 10 o'clock when we got the cycle running again and, five miles further on, about 15 from our destination, we had more tire trouble which could not be corrected. So we limped into the nearest town on a flat tire and, at midnight, while I was trying in vain to find a place to sleep, a French lieutenant came along. He was on the staff of a French general whose car he got and sent me on it. Thus, I arrived here about 2:00 a.m. Meantime, they had not expected me so there was no billet for me and I slept in bed with Blanks.

As it was, I beat the trucks in and the troops did not begin to arrive till morning and they found me back on the job. I told you how flattering to me it was their regret at my departure, but welcome back to me was even more so and officers and men flocked up to me and told me how glad they were to have me back again.

Here we are not in a sector but are back in rear training—You must have seen by now that this service is in alternate periods of line work and training.

I promised myself to be in bed tonight at 9:00 p.m. and it is nearly that now. The last few days have been very trying ones and I feel it.

Goodnight, Sweetheart—I love you—
Hugh

Life continued to be hard on Ida. On August 28, the day after Colonel Wise had received notice that he must report to the medical board, an event unknown to Ida, she wrote that she and the three boys were still moving around between the houses of friends and relatives and rooming houses. She reported that they had moved twelve times since leaving Camp Zachary Taylor, about six months before. She also wrote that she would be spending the winter in New York City at Miss Womword's lodging, that of $27 per week and no electricity, but gas, and shabby, dingy old furniture. She wrote, "How I wish I knew where you are tonight. . . . Oh, when will you be home and we be leading a normal happy life."

On September 20 Ida received Hugh's letter of August 31 and she replied:

Sept. 20th

My darling Husband

Your letter of August 31st came tonight. The last one before that was dated August 21st. All was well with you then but something dreadful must have happened in those ten days.

What was it? Why should you have been relieved from command of your regiment? What were the papers eventually found to be all right? Of course they were all right. Why didn't the inspector or whoever it was make sure something was wrong before he stirred every thing up? I know of course it was because of nothing wrong you had done but I can't bear to think of your being troubled and worried and not there to share it with you. Thank God the one letter which came says you are back in command of your regiment but it seems as if I couldn't wait for the others to come to tell me all about it. If you were Quartermaster I should think it some red tape laugh but I can't imagine what this can be. My heart aches for you although by now you have probably ceased being troubled by it. You wrote of being alone in the Hotel de France wondering what the next day would bring forth. Oh Sweetheart, I surely could have made it a little easier if only I could have been with you.

* * *

Sweetheart, I love you,

Ida

She continued to knit warm wool socks for her husband. Ineptly, but with dedication, the boys knitted a muffler. Her friends, who were less tied down with family, continued to volunteer for the Red Cross and drives to sell war bonds. Her days were full of children and her nights were lonely. She wrote Hugh every day. Her uncertainty and concern festered. Five days later she received the delayed mail and replied:

Sept 25th

My darling Husband

Today your letters of Aug 22, 27 and 28 came explaining the one of Aug 31st which I received nearly a week ago, and three more came, Sept. 1, 3 and 4. I have read and re-read them. I never thought of your leg being the cause of your being ordered away from your regiment because you said your papers were found all right and you were returned to the 61st. I have wondered and wondered what could be the trouble. How I wish I could have been with you when the sword finally fell. I think when you have your balance again, as you have long since I know, it will be a great relief to be able to admit that you have a bad leg and then go ahead. One of the most wearing parts of the trouble has been the constant attempt to conceal it and the fear of its being noticed. Now it has been noticed and mentioned but every one must realize how efficient your work has been in spite of it. So take a stick and be comfortable. I suppose the Brigade and Division Commanders were forced to report you as lame for an inspector would have asked why they didn't. I am so happy that you have a good friend like McAndrew where you can look for the best that he can give you. Evidently he avoided for you the Medical Board. I am glad for the trouble is so obscure and they might have fussed and called another board, etc. Did you show any one Pritchard's and the other reports? I wonder if you were returned to the 61st temporarily or only until the Staff Detail is ready for you.

You have had practically six months at the front, if a detail is given to you it seems the best thing possible. If Castner (Brigade Commander) or McMahon (Division Commander) are changed, the next general will do it all over again. Your cable has never come. Don't overdo your activity and thereby call the attention of Brig and Div Com'd'rs. I hope they won't think up some extra difficult piece of work to try you out, or did they seem satisfied when you were sent back? There are so many things I want to ask. I am glad you wrote as fully as you did. It wouldn't be fair not to. I think it was so kind of Lt. Berne to go with you. I would like to send wristlets or handkerchiefs or socks or something to him and Capt. Blanks and the man who gave you the shell for little Hugh, for a Christmas greeting. If you want them send a request. Also tell Capt. Blanks if his wife is still in New York to tell you where as I would like to see her again. I have told no one of your recent upheaval except Aunt Ida and Miss O'Neill. I am so glad Barney got to you for he is so sympathetic and devoted to you. Don't worry about your star. It is you the children and I love and while we would be delighted for you to have the gratification of the promotion, it wouldn't change you any. I never should like a star as I do my little eagle which I have worn every day. Plenty of time yet for you to get your generalcy, and if you don't, never mind a bit. Your last four letters seemed to show that you have rebounded as you always do and I am so glad. You know how happy I would be if you were given a detail in a less dangerous place. The affection shown you by your officers and men was very gratifying and I am so glad you wrote me of it. I wish so I could have been with you those hard days but the worst is over, the hidden is public and now you can save yourself some fatigue I hope.

Sweet heart, I love you, goodnight—Ida

As for the Lead Soldier, the upheaval of August 28–31 could not be discussed. As a scribe, he could only write as instructed and that was war, as usual. To the teller belongs the tale. On the 31st, he wrote:

31 August 18
Dear Hugh,

With the order relieving us and Rabadeau sector came orders to march to Raon-aux-Bois, in the Arches training area from which we were so suddenly hustled away to go to Moyen-moutier.

We are now scheduled to have the training in open warfare which was cut short then. I wonder if we shall have it this time or if some other emergency will arise to call us to the front again? We have lost about all confidence that anything will happen according to plan.

I think we were all glad to leave Moyenmoutier for, though it was comfortable and interesting, we were getting a bit "fed up" on trench warfare and this move looks like a step towards the "Big Push."

While we were at Moyenmoutier, some of the American troops got into the Chateau Thierry and the "Soissons" operations and distinguished themselves so our fellows began to feel that they had done their bit of trench war and "holding" work and that they should be let into the big game.

The night of August 20, a French battalion slipped into the trenches at Mère Henry and our battalion then slipped out and marched back to Etival. The next night, the same thing happened at La Forain. It was all done smoothly and quietly and the only incident was that a Boche avion caught a French column on the road and, swooping low, burnt them a little with machine gun fire before the antis drove it away.

On the morning of the 22nd, the Colonel turned over the command to the French colonel, mounted his horse and rode to Etival and that night the regiment was on its long march to the Arches area.

It was a beautiful march but a hard one because the men, after six weeks in the trenches, were in poor marching condition. As always, our marches were made at night. You can trace our route on your map. Our successive day halts were Jeanmenil, Girecourt, Cheminenil, Raon-aux-Bois.

We had a lot of rain on the march and our billets were by no means good but we arrived at our destination before day on August 26.

The next morning we started our training schedule, having devoted August 26 to the usual rites of billets, cooties and equipment.

But on August 26, orders came to move again and the next day the regiment piled into camions and trekked to the vicinity of Haussonville, South of Nancy. That is where we are now.

This is in the Toul sector of the "Big Battle" front. There is a feeling that we are going to do things—not simply hold a sector but drive forward and make the pace. Division after division of Americans are moving up this way and everyone believes there is to be a big American "push." We seem to be regarded now as graduates from the French-warfare class and we have heard that we are to be used as shock troops in the next "push." All of our training here is to be along those lines.

We are getting close, Hukins, and, unless I am much mistaken, I shall soon be writing you of big doings.

Goodnight,

Your Soldier

AT LAST, A SEPARATE
AMERICAN ARMY

FOLLOWING MARSHAL FOCH'S JULY 24 PLAN, ON AUGUST 8, 1918, the British forces, with some French support and an American infantry regiment that had been assigned to a British division, attacked between Montdidier and Albert. This was known as the Battle of Amiens, a railroad junction that linked Paris to the channel ports. The Germans had been camped four miles away, waiting for the opportunity to seize it. The Allied attack was an immediate and enormous success, pushing the Germans back ten miles. Although numbers differ, in a single day some 15,000 surrendered and within a week 33,000 had done so.[1] The number of German dead or wounded was staggering. The Allies used plentiful, fast, and awesome tanks that could not be matched or deterred by the Germans, although as the battle progressed most broke down.

Amiens confirmed that the Germans were in deep trouble and they knew it. On August 8, General Ludendorff famously wrote, "August 8 was the black day of the German army in the history of this war."[2] His distress was caused not only by the defeat, but also by the loss of morale among the German troops, who chose to surrender rather than fight. On August 13, Ludendorff told his nominal superior, General von Hindenberg, that the only course was a defensive one with occasional attacks in order to obtain favorable terms through negotiations. At a summit at Spa on August 13–14, Ludendorff was less candid with Kaiser Wilhelm II, but still told him that the war was a game of chance and must be ended. It was decided to extend peace feelers after the next success in the West. Nonetheless, the Germans were still not prepared to give up Belgium or Alsace-Lorraine.[3]

Following General Ludendorff's instructions, the army was engaged in only defensive actions and, even so, was losing. Troops leaving the front jeered at reserves replacing them, shouting epithets such as "strike-breakers" and "blacklegs." The reserves may have seemed to be only prolonging the war.[4] In reality, it was their leaders who were prolonging the war. The grieving and deprived German people were violently striking and, as in Britain, the German rulers were frightened that the unrest would lead to a Bolshevik-type revolution.

Even the ever-optimistic kaiser seemed anxious. His cousin the Russian tsar Nicholas Romanov had been deposed and executed. On September 1, Wilhelm II lectured to munition workers at the Krupp armament factory in Essen. Rattled, he explained that envy had induced their enemies to bring war to Germany, but God was the country's ultimate ally.

His withered arm behind him, invoking his version of the divine right of kings, the kaiser exhorted, "Each one of us has received his appointed task from on high. You at your hammer. You at your lathe, and I on my throne . . . and is it to be thought that the good God will abandon us there at the last moment? . . . We often at home and at the front and in the open air have sung 'A Mighty Fortress is our God'. . . . A nation from which such a hymn is originated must be invincible. Promise 'to fight and hold out to the last, so help us God.'"[5]

The war continued in the Vosges and elsewhere. American troops continued to pour into France, and the vexing question of how to deploy them was still unresolved. Not only was the last week of August 1918 pivotal for Colonel Wise individually, it was the turning point for General Pershing and the American forces and, hence, to the Colonel, as commander of the 61st Infantry. Even though there was now an official American army consisting of American soldiers and commanded by American officers, not all American troops were part of that army. The French and British were clamoring for those other troops, but the issue of amalgamation had been kicked down the road so many times that there had to be a showdown.

British general Sir Douglas Haig was under increasing pressure from home. Despite a magnificent government-sponsored propaganda campaign, people were questioning his leading their sons, husbands, and friends to senseless injury and death. To General Haig, the 1916 British defeat at the Battle of the Somme was transformed into a success because the enormous number of British casualties must have meant that the Germans had suffered equal losses.[6]

Not all shared Haig's belief that the greater the British losses the more successful the battle had been; nor did they share his thought that "We lament too much over death." He, himself, did not lament. He did not even permit himself to face the reality that might have caused him to understand why some softies did lament. Removed from the horrors of war, while sitting at his desk away from the front, Sir Douglas wrote to his son that he had refrained from visiting the casualty clearing stations because what he saw there made him physically ill.[7]

British prime minister Lloyd George wanted to dismiss Haig, but the general was as skilled as a politician as he was inept as a commander. He had friends in high places, including the king, and he was determined to stay on the job. Nonetheless, if he "smashed up" the present army, it would be his last.[8] The war, never popular with some, was becoming increasingly unpopular with many. Militant strikes by workers tired of the demands made of them for the war effort, but underpaid for those sacrifices, became more frequent. Most upsetting, especially to those in power, was the August 30 strike of the police, known as the "Bobbies," who served as the strikebreakers. Many British feared that a revolution, like that of the Bolsheviks in Russia, was coming.

Haig needed to have some victories without leading the British troops to slaughter and then tallying the casualties as the measure of success. Finally, he was finding some. The British followed up their victory at Amiens with more along the northern flank of the western front. American troops, attached to the British ranks, were helping and could provide the British with necessary replacements. Sir Douglas may have thought that it was better to squander American lives than to increase the British death toll.

In August, five American divisions either were in training behind the lines or had already fought under British command. Haig wanted to keep all those fresh faces. Nonetheless, on August 12, General Pershing refused to play along. He insisted that three of those divisions be removed from British command and placed with the new American army.[9] Reluctantly, Haig acquiesced.

The catalyst for resolution of the American-French-British amalgamation conflict was the St. Mihiel Salient, a 150–200-square-mile hernia-like German protrusion into French territory that had been captured by the Germans in 1914 and been a relatively quiet area since a French attempt to retake the area had failed in 1915. Just beyond the Salient lay the Woëvre plain and the crucial Mézières-Sedan-Metz railroad line and thirty-two miles farther was the city of Metz, a former French fortress city where Marshal Foch had been studying when the city fell to the Germans in 1870, during the Franco-Prussian war.

Since his arrival in France, Pershing had focused on "reducing" (the term of the day) this salient with an independent American force under his command. He had envisioned flattening the bulge and then proceeding to Metz, severing lateral rail connections and occupying crucial coal fields and iron-producing facilities.[10] On August 24, General Pershing met with Marshal Foch and the outline of the attack on the salient was drawn up. It did not include, however, following through to Metz, but the potential to do so was evident. The expected seasonal rain on the Woëvre plain was a potential problem.

The brunt of the attack was to be the assault by the American army from the south. On the western side of the salient, three or four American divisions with five or six French divisions would attack. The British had reneged on their promise to provide heavy tanks for the attack, but the French were to provide artillery and light Renault Whippet tanks.

On August 29, with appropriate ceremony, the French generals who had been in command there, dressed for the occasion in red trousers and blue coats, turned command of the St. Mihiel sector over to Pershing.[11] At last Black Jack's army, with him in control, would engage in a major battle and, if there were to be an attached force, it would be French and under American command. General Pershing had finally prevailed, or so it seemed.

The next day, August 30 (also the day that Colonel Wise had resumed command of the 61st Infantry and the British Bobbies went on strike), Foch called upon Pershing at his residence. Citing the recent Allied successes, he presented a new plan—one that would call for limiting the goals of the American attack on the salient. Upon attaining those objectives, the American forces would then be farmed out to the French forces for an attack farther to the north, where the war would be won.[12]

To Pershing, the revised plan meant prevention, or at least delay, of the formation of the American army, and "despite the contribution of our splendid units whatever success might be attained would be counted as the achievement of the French armies and our participation regarded as entirely secondary."[13] General Pershing objected. Marshal Foch challenged, "Do you wish to take part in the battle?" Pershing retorted, "Most assuredly, but as an American Army and in no other way."[14]

Heated conversation ensued. Provoked, General Pershing admonished, "Marshal Foch, you have no authority as Allied Commander-in-Chief to call upon me to yield up my command of the American Army and have it scattered among the Allied forces where it will not be an American army at all." Foch rejoined, "I must insist upon the arrangement." Black Jack, the poker player and teller of his tale, slammed back, "Marshal Foch, you may insist all you please, but I decline absolutely to agree to your plan. While our army will fight wherever you may decide, it will not fight except as an independent American army."[15] Foch left the table, picked up his maps and papers and, after handing the general a memorandum of his proposal, left. The following day, Pershing formally replied to the memorandum with his objections.[16]

On September 2, after emotions cooled, a compromise was reached that limited the scope of the St. Mihiel attack. Beginning September 10, the Americans would reduce the salient, apparently a foregone conclusion, and then immediately march north to engage in the Battle of Meuse-Argonne. The logistics of such a transition presented enormous obstacles and the toll on the soldiers was more than should have been demanded, but General Pershing had finally won against the British and the French. He had his American army, under his command, fighting a major battle, and then going forward to fight, as a unit, in what was envisioned to be the final battle. The American army would, at least, share the glory of final victory.

For Foch, if there was such a heated exchange between him and General Pershing on August 30, it did not merit mention in his memoirs. While acknowledging that he had changed the scope of the original plan for St. Mihiel, he stated, "I was led to ask General Pershing to undertake a new offensive."[17] He recounts that on September 2 he met with General Pershing and French general Pétain and a written note was prepared calling for the limited attack on St. Mihiel. Then between September

20 and 25, the American army would make an attack west of the Meuse River between the river and the Argonne woods, "supported on the left by an attack of the French Fourth Army, the whole under the command of General Pétain."

Because of logistical problems the St. Mihiel attack had to be delayed for two days, until September 12. In the interim, the American troops, including the 61st Infantry of the 5th Division, were gathering for the big show. Rounding up and placing the troops was done mostly at night and was a nightmare. From September 6–10, the Lead Soldier wrote:

6 September 18

It has been a busy week since I started this letter and we are in for another busy week for orders came today to move forward. We march from here as soon as it is dark. When I write that we are in a certain place or that we march at a certain time, you must not think of the whole regiment as being in that town. Few French country towns could hold a regiment. What I mean is that regimental headquarters and some of the troops are in the town which is in the middle of the regimental area and that the remainder, probably the greater part of the regiment, is billeted in nearby towns and villages.

* * *

The week here at Haussonville has been very profitable. It is a suitable place for the work we were doing and the men, realizing that it was their last chance to learn the open war game before they have to play it, have been eager and energetic.

Battalion and regimental maneuvers have been thorough and realistic and have been well-executed. In some of these we have had aeroplanes working with us and in all of them great stress has been laid on all means of communication and liaison by telegraph, telephone, wireless, tps (ground telegraphy), visual signaling, runners, pigeons, and every other possible means.

It is remarkable how the signal platoon keeps the Colonel, the majors and all the moving units in perfect touch. Liaison is one of the most important things in battle and important messages are usually sent in several ways. In one of our maneuvers, the Colonel got the same message in eight different ways—radio, tps, telegraph, telephone, flag, runner, aeroplane, and pigeon.

Also we have had instruction with fire grenades and "smoke pots." Fire grenades are fiendish things. They are fired from the muzzle of a rifle like the ordinary rifle grenade but when they burst they throw a spray of burning phosphorus and sulfur that reduces to cinders anything it lands on. The smoke pots make a dense cloud of low-hanging smoke to conceal the movement of troops behind it.

The Colonel has another horse now. He turned Roan over to his orderly sergeant and got a little Thoroughbred mare which he named Violu. She was hurt a few days later and now he has "Yvette" far and away the best of the three and a stunner for style and looks.

Here comes the Colonel now—he will take me from the table, drop me into his dispatch case, and it's joggle and shake for me all night.

10 September 18
Dear Hugh,

We have just finished another four days, or rather, four nights of marching—Haussonville, Champigneulle, Saizerais, X.

X is where we are now and we know of no other name for it. It was X on the march order and we were guided here so we need no name for it. When we do not call it X we call it "Balloon Woods" because it is in a small forest and there was a balloon company camped here when we arrived. The weather for the past few days has been simply atrocious, raw, cold and the rain falling in deluges. Last night's march was the worst I ever saw. The rain fell in sheets and the night was pot black but had it not been for the rain we should have in all probability had Boche aero bombs which would have been worse.

We are pretty close up to the lines now and these are the real lines for in front of us is the famous San Mihiel Salient which the Boche have held jutting into the French line for 4 years and which the French have not been able to retake.

It is very lively up in front and for the last ten miles along the road coming here we watched the sky ahead of us shimmering with gun and shell flashes as by heat lightning. Often we could see the flashes of the bursting shells, the glare of the star shells, and the trail of the signal rockets. All the time there was the low growl of the battle punctuated by the boom of the big guns. Just before we reached Balloon Woods one of our ammunition dumps, about a half-mile from the war was set off by a Boche shell and blew up. First there was a heavy explosion and then an explosion which fairly shook the earth and sent up thousands of shells and grenades bursting and crackling in the air like mammoth firecrackers. It was like some big set piece of fireworks but it was a thousand times bigger. The country for miles around was lighted by the flare and the concussion was almost terrifying. Poor Yvette was completely terrified—she squatted close to the ground and sprang straight up and then crouched trembling so that the Colonel thought she had been hit by one of the flying fragments. You can imagine how this felt to me in the dispatch case strapped to the saddle!

It is very easy for us to see that we are moving up to take part in something big—I wonder if the Americans are really going to try to smash the San Mihiel Salient! It looks that way!

For the last three days the French people have been telling our men that there was to be a big drive. Even the Colonel has received no official information of this but you can bet that the people are right. There is a saying that if one wants to get any confidential military information he has only to ask it of the lady in whose house he is billeted. They do seem to know and nothing delights them more than to chatter about what they know or what they think they know.

But that is just a little failing of the very estimable and splendid women.

The more one sees of the middle-aged women of these rural districts, the more he has to admire her. She is apt to be not very prepossessing in appearance and she is usually quite quiet and sad for her husband and sons are probably at the front or, perhaps, have been killed there. She is poor, has no servant and works like a slave to keep up a little garden and to maintain her house in good order and scrupulously clean. That makes me think of a queer thing about all of these French country towns—Inside, the houses are models of neatness and cleanliness, but out of doors, every rule of sanitation seems to be systematically violated. The squares are unkempt, the streets are dirty, and the yards are simply filthy. You can locate the homes of the well-to-do people because they, having more horses and cows, have the largest manure piles beneath their windows. On our march here, we passed through Nancy one night. Nancy is reputed to be one of the most beautifully picturesque cities of France and when you study French history you will learn how much of it centers there.

When we marched through the city it was pitch dark so we could only see the black masses of the buildings and the gables and towers outlined against the sky. Not a soul was on the streets and all doors and windows were tightly shut so no light could show out to guide Boche avions which frequently bomb the place. The city seemed uninhabited and one felt that he was riding through a dream of medieval times. Behind those tightly closed blinds we knew that there were people and we could imagine how their hearts jumped with joy as they listened to the tramp of thousands of American soldiers pushing forward through the storm to help save France.

Today we sent forward a detail of officers and non-commissioned officers to "Y" the name of which like that of "X" is not mentioned, even in orders. They will receive instructions for guiding the regiment when we move.

* * *

I cannot say much for "X" as a pleasure resort. The troops have bivouacked in their shelter tents camouflaged under the trees and bushes. It is still pouring rain and they are wet, cold and uncomfortable and mud! Stiff, sticky, yellow mud! Gooey mud!!! Almost knee deep everywhere! Wagons stall! Ration cart stuck! Ammunition carts hub deep and we are moving into battle but we will get there somehow!

Good Night,

Your Soldier

The American army was ready and willing. Whether it was able was still unknown, but now it was time to find out. Now, it was time to flatten the bulge of the St. Mihiel salient by the stomp of American boots, if they could just get those boots out of stiff, sticky, gooey yellow mud.

ELEVEN

ST. MIHIEL

C OLONEL WISE WAS ONE OF 550,000 AMERICAN SOLDIERS and 110,000 French who were going to attack the salient.[1] By that time, the 61st Infantry consisted of about 1,500 soldiers. The Colonel had pointed out to Ida that, when marching, the regiment stretched out for three miles, and yet it was a very small part of the whole. In support of the effort were to be 3,000 French artillery guns, manned by French and American soldiers; 267 French Whippet tanks, driven by French and American jockeys, one of whom was Lieutenant Colonel George Patton, who would be showered with glory in the next world war; and 1,500 French and British aircraft, some of which were flown by American pilots.[2] The attack was to begin on September 12.

The terrain was tough, especially for an attack from the south.[3] The heights of the hills of Montsec and Loupmont which were held by the Germans permitted superior observation of all that might threaten. The middle ground around Thiaucourt was pitted with craters from countless rounds of exploded artillery shells. The Woëvre plain was already swampy from rain. Unmapped and unknown streams meandered through the salient without pattern.

The Germans had availed themselves of the relative calm over the years and had occupied themselves with fortifying their trenches and artillery-proofing their shelters. They built amenities and cultivated vegetable gardens.[4] They were well entrenched. Yet their numbers, approximately 75,000,[5] were small relative to the masses forming to attack.

Despite French and American attempts to spread false rumors about where an offensive was going, the Germans knew that the salient was the target. They originally thought that the attack would only be from the south, and their strategy was to permit an initial American breakthrough into the Woëvre and then counterattack.[6] On September 9, their command became aware that the western flank would also be assailed, which would render their plan ineffective. Unknown to the Allies, their foe began to withdraw the following day.

On September 11, 1918, the day before the attack, the Lead Soldier wrote:

11 September 18

Dear Hugh,

Now we know where "Y" is we know what is to be our job—the Americans have been assigned the task of flattening the San Mihiel Salient and "Y" is the position from which we "take off" in the attack. I guess they call it "Y" because it is next to the last and the last will be "Z"—the last of the San Mihiel Salient, anyway.

When that is gone, the great fortified city of Metz will fall easily—it will be just "etc."

This afternoon, when the Colonel came back from brigade headquarters, he sent for the battalion commanders and the staff. Having spread out the maps, he went over with them the entire situation. When all clearly understood this, he dictated to them an order.

* * *

The meeting broke up and the Colonel mounted Yvette and rode off with a part of the staff towards "Y."

It was dark soon after we started and it was a black, blustery night, the wind howling and the rain coming down in sheets.

For several miles our route was along a trail through the woods fetlock deep with oozy slippery mud so the horses could hardly keep on their feet. Then we came out onto a better road which, like all the roads leading our way, was full of moving troops pushing forward through the rain and darkness. It is fortunate that it was such a bad night for what a chance it would have been for Boche avions!

These troops were, like us, the local reserves coming into their positions. Their forward echelons, like our other brigade, were already in position awaiting the H hour and the big general reserve, a day's march in the rear was following up to take over what we gain and to push on further.

Now we begin to see where all the artillery that had been rolling forward for days had been going—behind every knoll, beneath every embankment—everywhere, there were batteries—big guns, middle-sized guns, little 75's—in some places sit almost hub to hub—literally miles of guns awaiting the H minus four hours.

As we rode along, the Colonel said to the adjutant: "Captain, I didn't think there was as many guns in the world." "No, sir, but I'm glad to see them there" replied the adjutant.

When we got nearly to Mamey we were stopped by the military police who informed us that we could not pass there because the Boche was shelling Mamey and had run some of our artillery out of there.

So, after some remarks that do not bear writing, the Colonel started on a long detour and in making that, we got mixed up with an artillery regiment moving our way and an ammunition truck train hurrying back to the rear to refill. A truck train in a hurry on a dark road without lights is not a pleasant thing to meet and it was particularly disagreeable when one has to ride between it and a column of guns also on the move.

How those truck drivers get around as they do over these congested roads, in inky darkness without lights is a wonder but they do and most of their travel is at night.

The "old man" was greatly worried about the shelling of Mamey because the route of our regiment was through there and he was afraid it might be late getting into position or that the Boche might catch it on the road. They did shell the road just before our column reached there but only a few shells came near our troops.

But Fritz was feeling all around behind our lines tonight with his artillery and he killed a lot of men and horses.

Such a jam as there was on all roads you just have to imagine but the tide swept on towards the Boche barrier which it was destined to sweep away.

We have our little covered niche in the hillside here for our PC and are as snug as a bug in a rug. It is nearly midnight now— the Colonel is out in the road waiting for the regiment to arrive.

Good Night,

Your Soldier

As scheduled, on September 12, the St. Mihiel offensive began. The Lead Soldier reported:

12 September 18

Dear Hugh,

While I am writing you this, one of the most important battles of this greatest of wars is waging around us. We are of it and in it but, so far, our regiment has taken no part in the actual fighting and has suffered only a few casualties, those from shells.

Like an actor, we are standing in the wings, watching the play and awaiting the cue that will call us onto the stage.

The regiment arrived on time and took its position in the support. Our liaison within the regiment and with other organizations was established. Telephone and telegraph lines were strung out, trains of relay runners established, visual signal apparatus placed, wireless poles run up, and the pigeon coops distributed so that communication between regimental headquarters and the division, brigade and battalions could not fail.

Re-supply of ammunition and rations was provided for. Arrangements were made for the care of the dead and wounded and for the handling of prisoners—and a hundred other details that were or might become necessary.

One by one the officers charged with attending to these things reported them done, and, before the H-hour, the Colonel reported "Ready."

Meantime, our other brigade was in the forward trenches, ready to "jump off." Four hours before the H-hour arrived, while our infantry was still struggling through the mud to its positions, punctually as the watch ticked 1 o'clock am our artillery opened the battle which, I heard the Colonel tell the adjutant, is the beginning of the final phase of the war. He says of course we will win this fight and that will mean the downfall of Metz soon after. But what makes the battle important is that this is a purely American offensive and the moral effect of a great victory by the newest entrant into the war will be tremendous. After this fight the German people can be no longer deceived as to America's strength and sympathies. The Kaiser will have to admit that he overestimated the time necessary for us to become a factor and that he underestimated our power.

At 1 o'clock am, above nature's storm burst another storm which drowned out nature's storm from then til 10 o'clock am, our heavy artillery, along a 15 kilometer front, pounded the Boche. It hammered not only his forward lines, to drive him to cover, and his artillery, to prevent its counterfire, but also his reserve positions and the roads leading forward from them so the Boche could not support nor reinforce his line nor withdraw troops from it.

His command post, his ammunition dumps, his supply dumps, and all other sensitive points were unmercifully pounded to disorganize his system of command and supply. For four hours this terrific bombardment continued—a thousand heavy guns; 125's, 175's, 6-inch, 8-inch, and even 14 inch, threw hundreds of tons of projectiles hurtling over us to land on the spots where Fritz wanted them least but which our intelligence service had worked weeks to locate.

Now and again the Boche guns tried to reply but immediately our counter-battery guns would smother them.

The whole affair had opened so suddenly and so furiously and so powerfully that the Boche artillery was carried off its feet and it could not regain them—it simply did not have a chance and this must have been particularly bitter for the Boche because he is in the habit of more than holding his own in the artillery phases of battle.

Well Hukins! It was grand! A fellow just wanted to jump up and shout for joy!

The four hours went by like four minutes without a cessation or diminution of the crash and whir and roar—shrapnel, high explosives, or gas went over to Fritz in every one of those thousands upon thousands of chugging, whining, sizzling projectiles and he was reaping what he had sowed and getting a bully good crop at that.

Up til the H-hour, the four hours of fire had been fired in preparation of the assault, primarily the job of the heavies. So, while the heavies were chanting their song, more than a thousand 75's sat quietly "keeping cool" and waiting to join the chorus. It was the function of the 75's to furnish the accompanying barrage for the infantry assault.

No watch was needed to tell when 5 o'clock am arrived for simultaneously every 75 greeted it and as gray dawn changed to gray day, the crash, bang, boom of the preparation fire was swelled into a mighty roar by the addition of the 75's firing at top speed to roll their barrage ahead of the infantry advance.

It was no longer the pulsating boom of big guns and the intermittent rush as the freight trains overhead—the explosive noise was now one continuous c-r-a-s-h and, above, was the roar of Niagara.

ST. MIHIEL SALIENT
1918

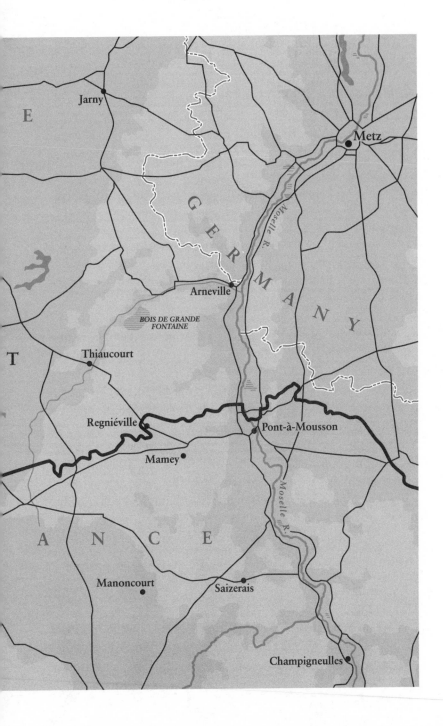

The sky of a gray dawn was turned crimson by the gun flashes in no man's land which, a few seconds before, was in hazy darkness was now in bright illumination from the bursting shells which formed a flickering line of flame that crept forward like a prairie fire towards the Boche trenches.

Following 200 yards behind that line of fire we knew were the infantrymen with a fire in their hearts even more dangerous to the Boche than the shellfire and that in their hands were the bayonets that would prod Fritz out of the cover that protected him from the barrage. We felt very idle as we stood and watched this fight but, of course, we were doing our part and we all know there will be work for us, probably worse than this for when we leapfrog the other brigade and go forward we shall not have such a splendid artillery support. I will write you later.

Your Soldier

While the 61st Infantry stood by and watched the fight, waiting its turn, others were deep into the fray, but it was not much of a fray, except for those killed or wounded. From an overview such as that which General Pershing enjoyed from heights south of the battle, all was going remarkably well. Against limited resistance, objectives sought to be attained the following day were achieved the first morning. The Americans had thought up the innovation of placing chicken wire on top of the otherwise-impenetrable masses of barbed wire and then walking across.[7] They might have been targets, but the Germans had either withdrawn or were surrendering in droves.

On September 13, while Colonel Wise's regiment was still in reserve, The Lead Soldier wrote:

13 September 18
Dear Hugh,

I am no more suspicious than other soldiers but I am glad we made our attack yesterday instead of today which is Friday the Thirteenth. Anyway, everything has gone fine and our attack has carried its objectives all along the line. The American advance has been so rapid and so determined that they have been in danger of getting away from their ammunition supply and the supply companies of the advancing troops have not been able to properly ration them. The troops in rear have had to come to their assistance with their ammunition carts and supply trains and have had to make large carrying details to get ammunition and food forward from points where wheeled transport had to stop.

All day, hundreds of prisoners have been herded past us on the way to the rear and the litter-bearers and ambulances are going back in a steady stream with the wounded, American and Boche.

MANY HINDSIGHTERS, such as historians necessarily are, have relegated the reduction of the St. Mihiel salient from a military battle to a walkover. Even at the time, a prevalent thought was that the Americans had not so much won a victory as "relieved" the Germans in the salient. The on-site observations of the Lead Soldier, as he continued his letter of September 13, cast doubt upon that facile assessment:

Tonight our regiment began to move up. The second battalion advanced and took position close behind the regiment of the other brigade which we will relieve. The first battalion closed up behind the second battalion and the third battalion is behind the first—all nosing up to be in springing distance.

Our PC came forward to just south of Regnieville, between the First and Third battalions.

Coming forward we passed over the ground where yesterday's assault was made. What a tangled mess of disorder it was! The ground was all plowed up and pitted with shell holes, the Boche trenches were caved in and, in places, obliterated. Wrecked tanks, smashed gun carriages, broken down ammunition carts, rifles, equipment, helmets and clothing—everywhere!

Unexploded grenades and dud shells made it necessary to watch one's step or his horse's step. Dead lay along the roads and dead men were in the trenches in between them.

The salvage corps was already at work collecting property and details were burying the dead and burning the dead horses.

Having inspected the battalion positions, the Colonel came to our new PC which was by this time all connected up and in liaison. But, tonight, we are keeping both this PC and our last one in operation to be sure that confusion may not result from our late change. This is a rather dreadful place, this PC. It is dark and damp and dirty. The staff officers have named it "The Potato Cellar," and it is like one. It is better though than the driving rain outside. It was a Boche dugout and, as usual, they left their reminders. We have all been scratching cooties and throwing things at rats ever since we arrived.

Reilley and Hall have come up with a gunney sack of rations and they are making coffee and frying bacon on an old Boche stove. We will have supper soon unless the Boche thoughtfully left a grenade as he often does.

Good Night,
Your Soldier

A popular perception has been that the Battle of St. Mihiel was over after September 13. On that day, Generals Pershing and Pétain had gone to the liberated town of St. Mihiel.[8] It was also General Pershing's birthday and he felt properly self-congratulatory. There was, however, still work to be done and the front was far less appealing than was the scene at the St. Mihiel town site, which by then was behind the lines. On September 14, the Lead Soldier wrote:

14 September 18
Dear Hugh,
    Last night while the Colonel and his staff were squatted around Riley's stove, like a band of Commanches, the sergeant

said that he had a hunch that something would happen in the morning—"I know darned well something will happen in the morning and every other morning in this game" replied the signal officer, over his tin can of coffee.

But I'll bet that neither of them suspected what would happen for it is such an unusual thing that we had forgotten its possibility—the sun came out!—the glorious warm sun to dry these poor, wet, shivering men! It was so pleasant and bright when we came out of the potato cellar that we stayed out and brought the telephone out with us. It was one of those warm, balmy, lazy mornings that makes a fellow feel like loafing and, after the wet and cold and work of the past week; we would have been willing to sit on ammunition boxes by the cellar door and do nothing but bask in the sunshine. But, in this war business, basking in the sunshine is not on the schedule.

Most of the staff were already off on their various duties and soon all the others were gone but the Colonel, the adjutant, and the sergeant. A telephone message to tell the Colonel that important orders were on the way to him and while he was waiting for them he was improving the shining hour by having a much needed shave. The adjutant was checking off yesterday's casualty reports and the sergeant was overhauling his emergency case.

In the little valley just below us the headquarters company were drying their clothes and, "reading their shirts."—You do not know what that means, do you?—Well guess!—It's the same as hunting "seam squirrels!"

Over across the valley, about a half-mile in the rear of us, three big captive balloons swung lazily back and forth on their cables—about a thousand feet up, taking observations on the Boche lines, while around them and above them, a dozen of our planes circled and flitted to protect them from Boche avions. Suddenly, one of our orderlies shouted: Look! And stood pointing to a shiny object, dropping out of the blue sky—"a Boche!" said all three officers at once. Down he came! Almost straight down! Right through the circle of guard planes! Then, righting himself, he headed for the nearest balloon "tac-tac-tac, tac-tac-tac. Tac-tac-tac" went his machine gun and a stream of incendiary bullets ripped through the gas bag. Out of the basket popped the aeronaut on a parachute as the balloon burst into flames and sank burning towards the ground. "Tac-tac-tac, tac-tac-tac" and the same thing was repeated at the next balloon. "Tac-tac-tac, tac, tac, tac," and again it happed to the third balloon.

It had all taken less time than was needed to write about it. In less than a minute after we first saw the Boche plane, our three balloons were in flames and the observers were floating earthward on parachutes and Fritz, having finished his job, was headed for home as fast as his wings could carry him which was fast enough to elude the guard planes that tried to head him off. As he came over us, the Colonel, standing on a box, his face still lathered was waving his razor in the air and shouting to headquarters company: "Give it to him, men. Give it to him."

There was a fuselade but Fritz kept on. By this time several antis got busy but Fritz flew on outstripping several of our machines that gave him chase and squirting his machine gun on a column of troops on the road over which he flew.

"That fellow ought to have a bushel of iron crosses," said the Colonel as he picked up his razor which he had dropped—"darn him! He's made me break my only razor!"

That Boche certainly put one over on our planes—he simply went so high that they did not heed him until it was too late. Then he dropped like a plummet right into their midst and downed the balloons they were guarding before they could turn to their assistance. It was a pretty plan, daringly executed and the true test is that it succeeded.

But this was only one of the air combats we saw today for there have been a dozen of them right around us. Our planes are trying to locate the new positions of the Boche and his planes are trying to prevent this reconnaissance and to discover the roots and the strength of our troops coming forward.

This has resulted in constant contention for "the right of way" in the air. Some of the flights have been single combats one against one—other fights have been between a number of planes on each side. Sometimes two planes starting a fight would be joined by others until there was a flock of them fighting and we, on the ground, could not tell which were ours and which were Boches. There have been a lot of planes on both sides down here today, two right in front of our PC.

The Boche has one kind of plane that is a terror—a little red-nosed devil with stubby wings. It seems to be faster and handier than any of the others. This kind seems to travel in squadrons and we hate to see them come over because, so far, they have nearly always gotten the best of the fight.

It is maddening to have to stand on the ground and watch these airfights without being able to help our planes—especially if the Boche planes in a scrap happen to outnumber ours.

In my letter to you yesterday, I did not tell you much about the tanks. There were a lot of them in the assault but they had a hard time of it. The ground was such a mire of oozing mud that the tanks could not, as a rule, keep up with the infantry and dozens of them got stuck. Most of them were the little French "whippets" carrying a machine gun or two or a 75. These cannot go where the big tanks could go and the wide trenches with muddy sides stopped them.

I have mentioned Regnieville several times. I wish you could see it for then you would understand what a town is like after a battle has swept over it. There is not a roof left and few walls are standing. What was Regnieville is now about 10 acres of stone heaps and debris and we are taking away the stone to repair the roads.

It is very sad to look at this desolate ruin of what was once a pretty town with its churches, theaters, market, stores, and homes. One can hardly climb through the streets now over the piles of wreckage. The yards and gardens are buried deep under broken furniture, stones and mortar.

One looks at it and thinks what a sweet, peaceful place it must have been before the Kaiser started to "kulture" France.

Not a dog nor a cat is in that town—not a living thing in that devastated place which was alive with thrifty men and women and happy children. And this is only one of many towns like it in this section and this section is only a small part of the devastation the Boche has caused.

Thank God, he will be beaten and his "kulture" will be stopped before it reaches America!

It is not a lead soldier's job to preach about civilization and Christianity but a lead soldier knows more about them than does a Boche.

Today, the fight up forward has continued. Our leading brigade, having won it objectives, has been organizing its position. Its advance towards the end was not so rapid as at first for the further it progressed the more difficult was the artillery's task to aid and support it. Taking advantage of this the Boche was able to regain its feet and his resistance became more stubborn til, finally, he has stopped pulling back and is making a stand on the hills of Bois de Grande Fontaine. Also, he is bringing up reserves and his guns are heavily shelling our forward positions. In our rapid advance, we have gotten away from our guns and closer to his and the difficulty of getting our guns forward has passed the artillery advantage to the Boche. So our troops, in holding their gains, are having a harder fight than they had in their advance.

They have done their part most handsomely and now they are pretty well played out and it will be our task to take over the fight for them.

That is what the soldiers call "passing the hot brick." They would much prefer to go over the top in the first assault with the sufficient artillery support than to come in later as we are about to do. You see, before a prepared assault everything is known of the enemies' position and all arrangements are made to assist and support it—the waves bounce out of the trenches and follow their barrage over the Boche trenches and there is excitement and exhilaration in it. But later, when the enemy has recovered from the demoralization caused by our barrage and, out of reach of our prepared artillery positions, he turns for a stubborn stand, it is quite another matter and he is liable to have the edge on us. They are quite sure to have to withstand a furious bombardment that he has prepared and resist a counter-attack with a weakened artillery to support us. The important order we were waiting for this morning was the order to take over "the hot brick"—to leapfrog the regiment ahead of us, drive forward to the "exploitation line" and dig in.

So long,

Your Soldier

So far, the 61st Infantry had been part of the chorus at the big show, or perhaps, had not even come onto the stage. To many, there had not even been a big show. Historian Gary Mead has written that after September 13 the Germans counter-attacked several times in "a desultory, half-hearted fashion."[9] He reported that "The prisoner bag was satisfactory without being enormous: just 16,000 Germans fell into the hands of the A.E.F. [Americans]." He opined, "But the A.E.F. struck lucky at St. Mihiel, and never again had such a cake-walk." A "cakewalk" can be described as "an easy time." According to *Webster's Dictionary*, "the term originates from black American entertainment contests where a cake is the prize for the most accomplished steps in walking or stage dancing."

The Lead Soldier reported from the front on September 15 and 16, as follows:

15 September 18

Dear Hugh,

Last night our battalions began to move in and take over this "hot brick" which has not cooled off at all today.

With some hard fighting we have pushed our leading battalion well beyond the army objective into the Bois de Grande

Fontaine and tonight our PC is in the former PC of a Boche regiment, in the north edge of the Bois Saint Claude.

The Boche had been here a long time and they have made themselves quite comfortable. This command post of theirs was no dirty hole simply for occupancy during a fight but really a beautiful and comfortable place to live in. It is just behind the crest of a large gently sloping hill about a mile north of what was their front line. It was quite well protected from fire from that direction, from which we came, but it is not at all so from fire from the north in which direction the Boche now is.

It is a regular little village of dugouts that open upon streets which are deep winding trenches floored with neat boardwalks and artistically revetted with fir posts stood on end. The streets are nicely graded and one passed from one level to another by pretty little rustic stairways. The grounds in between these streets is made pretty by landscape gardening and there are even flower beds and ornamental shrubbery. There is a fine officer's mess, a club house, a pavilion, and all together, it is more like a summer resort than a command post.

But, inside the dugouts, one sees that they were constructed with as careful consideration for safety as the outside was made for beauty. There are dugouts for the different regimental offices, all thoroughly furnished and equipped, lighted by electricity, and connected with the field telephones and telegraphs and there are ample accommodations for the officers and enlisted personnel of a regimental headquarters—all of them most luxuriously furnished. At Brial, we thought the French had fixed themselves up quite well but their arrangements did not compare with this for comfort and convenience.

The only trouble with it is that everything faces the wrong way—the Boche was protected from the French shells but we have no hill between us and the Boche and their dugouts all open towards him. Of course, having occupied this village for a long time, he is quite familiar with it and he occasionally drops in a shell with most annoying accuracy.

He was run out of here in such a hurry that he did not have much time to prepare the place for us but, nevertheless, we were cautious as ever against his boobytraps taking no chances till our searchers had thoroughly examined the whole place. However innocent things may appear, one never knows what may be a trap—your weight on a step may detonate a mine and blow up the dugout. Moving a chair, hanging a coat on a peg in the wall, picking up a paperweight from the table or doing some equally natural and simple thing may make the electrical connection that causes a terrific explosion.

Careful examination shows plainly that the Boche had left in too great a hurry to prepare any welcoming fireworks for us—in fact, he left some of the food in his officers mess and our officers ate it, though only the tinned stuff whose seals showed it could not have been tampered with. These tins were labeled "For export to Holland" and our first meal in the Boche trenches was on Ritters Pork and Beans and George Washington coffee, hospitably left us by the Boche.

The second battalion was assigned the duties leading off with our attack. The Colonel gave the Major final instructions and at dark last night it moved forward.

Deploying in rear of the troops it was to relieve, it leapfrogged them and drove forward against the Boche in Grande Fontaine while the first and third battalions came up and took position half a kilometer behind it. A stiff fight ensued but we carried the position and began to dig in.

16 September 18

Twice last night the Boche gave us a terrific bombardment and they followed up, the second time, with a vigorous infantry assault that was handsomely beaten back. His showing today has been almost continuous and has frequently risen to fierce intensity.

Several times he has tried with his infantry to retake the ground we have gained so fighting has been bitter and bloody.

Once the second battalion was forced to give ground, but it fell back fighting. The Boche followed up its withdrawal and re-occupied the ridge. Then two companies, each of the First and Third battalions were sent in to support the second battalion and again we took the lost ground and with it we captured a large number of prisoners and machine guns. One company captured 16 machine guns and a lot of ammunition and the company commander manned the captured guns with his men and turned them on the Boche.

After a day of continuous and bitter fighting, night found us in possession of the ground we were assigned to take.

Early in the night, the Boche rolled a barrage over us and made another vigorous attempt to retake the position but he failed again and he paid heavily for it.

All day, he has been lavish with gas, especially tonight and the woods reek of it.

The Colonel has just come back from the Second Battalion and I heard him say to the Adjutant: "It's all right—we are holding and we are going to hold and we can go forward too!" Reilley brought him a good supper and, judging by the way he went after that, his appetite has been hurt by no lack of confidence.

"How can you eat in the midst of all this?" asked the surgeon—"Don't I need it?" replied the old man—"Yes" said the surgeon, "but I never have an appetite while I'm uneasy." "Oh Thunder!" replied the Colonel—"That was earlier in the day— I'm not uneasy now Doctor—my patient is past danger—he's getting well—weller every minute—Thank you—He's out of danger—Why, the Boche is busted! His counter has failed!— He's licked!" Then, to the Adjutant, "Captain, I haven't had a wink of sleep for two days—call me in an hour or before that if anything happens." Rolling over on a Boche bed, he was in two minutes sound asleep.

Good Night,
Your Soldier

On September17, the Lead Soldier wrote:

17 September 18

Dear Hugh,

The old man did not get that hour's nap, for before the hour was up, the leading troops of the regiment of a division from the general reserve arrived to relieve us.

* * *

In spite of all precautions to avoid a mix up, it was of course next to impossible to prevent some confusion; especially since right in the midst of the relief the Boche broke out with another terrific strafing of our position and even attempted to push forward into it again. This brought about a lively fight in the very midst of our change but he was beaten back and our relief was effected without serious trouble.

By daylight, our regiment was all out and on its way back to its assembly place. Some of our officers were left to remain 24 hours in the lines with the new colonel. Our Colonel remained with him till noon and then handed over the "hot brick." Then we rode back to the Potato Cellar where the regiment was assembling.

Here we received order to march, after dark, to the Manoncourt area for rest and training! We certainly need the one and we shall certainly get the other.

So there is our story of the Battle of St. Mihiel. The reduction of the St. Mihiel Salient is an accomplished fact. It is as flat as a pancake and the only Boche in it are dead or prisoners.

Our railroad artillery has moved up and is shelling Metz.

For the four years the Boche has held that salient and it had come to be regarded as redoubtable but now it is gone and our lines extend straight across what used to be the base of the triangle.

We have had to pay the price for the job but our losses have not been as heavy as the Boche losses and we have captured nearly 20,000 prisoners, nearly 500 guns, and heaven knows how many machine guns and other plunder.

Metz is under fire of our big guns and can be taken whenever we decide to pinch it off.

But most important of all is the moral effect of this great American victory. Heretofore, we have been operating with the French or the British and have had no sector of our own as we now have from Port-Sur-Seille to Verdun. This St. Mihiel entertainment was our own party in our sector.

By it, our Allies can see that America can be depended upon as a powerful and capable aid in our common cause and the Boche must realize what a dangerous and fast growing foe we are.

My letters, till recently, have been mainly about minor operations and the training that prepared us for the big game we are now playing in—and it is a big game for there were a million men in this battle which makes the greatest American battle, Gettysburg, look very small. Seven full divisions, over 200,000 men went forward with our assault. That is more men than Meade and Lee, together, had at Gettysburg and the armies with which Napoleon overran Europe rarely equaled the size of our reserve.

The ammunition burned in this one battle was probably more than the supply for any year of the Civil War and the prisoners we took outnumbered Shafter's army at Santiago.

Think of it: There were more men in this battle than there are men of draft age in greater New York. It would require a hundred big American box cars to haul a day's food for them and another to haul the ammunition for a day's fighting and hundreds more for forage, other supplies, and equipment. This will give you just an idea of the immense task that it is to prepare an operation like this which involves the assembling of a million and a half troops, the heavy and light artillery, aircraft, tanks, transport, supplies, sanitary service, etc., etc. The locating and establishment of hospitals, ammunition and ration dumps—organization of railheads and even the building of railroads.

And all of this had to be done in the face of a powerful, aggressive, alert enemy whose business it was to prevent or to spoil it all.

But it is done—that job is finished and so is the St. Mihiel Salient.

Good Night,
Your Soldier

Was it a desultory, half-hearted counterattack? Was it a cake-walk? That is what historian Gary Mead would have us believe. The Lead Soldier thought that the 61st Infantry would follow through to Metz. Citing General George Marshall, Mead suggests that Foch should not have cut short that original Pershing plan. Mead posits that if Pershing had taken Metz, the war would have been quickly over, with the Americans lauded as the great heroes.[10] Historian David Stevenson writes, "However, once the salient had been eliminated the attack was closed down, which was almost certainly a mistake on Foch's part but one that mattered relatively little at this stage."[11] Perhaps not in the final outcome, but I believe that what ensued did matter. However, to the teller belongs the tale.

In his diary, following a visit to the salient a month after conclusion of the attack, General Bullard tells the tale of the salient as follows:

> Yesterday and to-day, I passed through French villages that had been for four years in the hands of the Germans. A few unfortunate women had been left there during the German occupation. Their stories, their sufferings were sad, unprotected as they were against German brutality and lust. . . .
>
> As I passed over quiet areas of beautiful country utterly destroyed by the enemy, as I saw great forests killed as men are killed by shell and shrapnel, as I saw the infinite pains and labour to accomplish all this to hurt his enemy and protect himself, I was tremendously impressed with the German's will to conquer, his great determination and infinite patience. I saw hundreds of miles of trenches revetted with wood, stone, and cement, thousands of dugouts made almost as great and complete as houses; roads, houses, railroads, and miles and miles

of wire entanglements. It looked like the work of a world, and it is all wasted in so far as any material return is concerned—a deeply impressive sight.

Villages for many miles, about four miles on both sides of No Man's Land, have been utterly destroyed. The country cannot recover for a hundred years. When we shall have beaten the Germans and are making terms, those who are in charge of imposing our terms should be required to visit and see the country which German ambition and savagery have desolated. It would harden their hearts and exact justice from those barbarians. They have utterly torn up and desolated all the villages that they have occupied.[12]

Meanwhile, telling her own tale, on September 16, Ida had returned to New York City with the three boys after her summer of shuffling between relatives and friends. They took up residence at the rooms of Miss Momword, once again annoyed at the shabbiness of the place and at having no telephone. Electricity and gas lighting scarcely allowed reading at night. Hugh's letters of the end of August describing his ordeal of losing and then regaining command of his regiment would not begin to arrive for another four days. All Ida knew of St. Mihiel was from newspaper reports.

TWELVE

MEUSE-ARGONNE

WHEN GENERAL JOHN J. PERSHING MADE HIS compromise deal with Marshal Foch on September 2, 1918, his "can do" optimism imposed an enormous burden on the American fighters, staff, and support personnel. The first obstacle was getting to the Argonne forest: 600,000 troops, 2,700 artillery guns, accompanying horses, and supplies had to be moved at night over three roads a distance of sixty miles.[1] They were to be joined by other divisions that had not been engaged at St. Mihiel. Colonel George C. Marshall, Jr., who was to gain accolades in the next war and thereafter to lend his name to the rebuilding of Europe after that conflagration, orchestrated the effort. Eventually, 1,200,000 American soldiers and support personnel participated in what became known as the Meuse–Argonne offensive, which lasted the remaining forty-seven days of the war.[2]

Getting to the American sector had been the first obstacle. The next was the terrain. Historian Nick Lloyd described the area as follows: "They moved into difficult terrain. On their left lay the Argonne forest, a nightmare of thick woodland, hidden defiles and thin, winding tracks. In the centre the country was more open, with scattered woods and hills, but it was dominated by the forbidding rise of Montfaucon, bristling with defenses and an ideal observation point from which to spy on any attacker. On the right, the dominating heights on the far bank of the Meuse also allowed oblique fire to be directed on any Allied advance."[3]

The German defenses were formidable. Taking advantage of the difficult terrain, they had established four successive lines of defense, the last being the Hindenburg Line. They had placed, "dugouts, trenches, concrete emplacements, jungles of barbed wire, well-concealed machine-gun pits with perfectly interlocking fields of fire, and heavily camouflaged artillery positions."[4]

Not only did the troops need to travel to their positions on the lines, but so did all the necessary supplies. The roads were atrocious. Transportation was by "primitive motor trucks and especially on horse- and mule-drawn wagons," but there was a shortage of both and the condition of the horses and mules was bad, causing them to break down.[5] Congestion was a terrible problem. General Bullard describes the roads as follows:

> As we passed over this distance in the first day's attack there was no sign of this road (a pre-war road shown on maps) except stones scattered in two or three years' ploughing by the enemy's great guns. . . . The workmen formed practically a continuous line on both sides of the road and swarmed back of the side lines, like ants, gathering gravel and broken stone to be thrown upon the roadbed. . . . They could use only the lightest implements, because their trains with the heavier tools could not be brought for some time upon the ground. The men gathered stones by hand and brought them to the roadbed where they sank in the mud of late shell craters almost as if they had been dropped into a bottomless sea, so soft was the ground and so destructive the passage of vehicles. It was an exhausting, heart-breaking, discouraging, ever-continuous operation.[6]

Historian Lloyd observed, "Perhaps inevitably, this sector had been quiet for some time, with many French commanders regarding military operations here as nothing short of suicidal."[7] It was here that Foch assigned the Americans, after rejecting the General Pershing plan for the Americans to proceed from the St. Mihiel salient on to Metz.

Compounding the problem, the first American troops involved in the battle were very inexperienced and undertrained, to the extent that some may not have even known how to load a gun or throw a grenade.[8] The more experienced troops coming from St. Mihiel were not yet rested. The rain did not cease. Flu was rampant. Conditions were abominable.

The first goal of the Americans was to capture the Montfaucon Hill, on which the town of that name perched. In defense, the Germans could fire on all trying to ascend. On September 26, 1918, an artillery bombardment began, following which the Americans tried to swarm forward. Resistance was fierce and the attack did not go well.

Montfaucon did not fall until the next afternoon. Casualties were far more than had been expected. The whole American offensive bogged down in mud from the constant rain which slowed the delivery of necessary supplies over the inadequate roads. Confusion was followed by chaos. In four days the troops had advanced only about seven miles. With 45,000 casualties, "Whether he liked it or not, Pershing was now involved in a brutal attritional slog."[9] On September 30, the offensive was halted.

On September 29, French prime minister Clémenceau, *le Tigre*, had attempted to visit the demolished town of Montfaucon. He was unable to do so, because the roads were clogged, and became irate. Criticism cascaded on General Pershing from all sides. The Tiger roared that the American commander should be fired. Others railed that the Americans were not doing their part in the overall advance.

On October 3, Foch came up with a new plan, which Pershing thought originated from Clémenceau, to transfer some

American troops to French command.[10] Foch wrote that he and General Pétain came up with the idea as a way to save time and expedite a conclusion to the war.[11] Pershing summarily rejected the new attempt at amalgamation. Later, the Tiger forcefully denounced Foch for not having contacted President Wilson at that time to demand that Pershing be removed, deriding the general's "invincible obstinacy."[12] In contrast, on September 27, the British had begun their offensive to the north and two days later broke through the Hindenburg Line, but the Americans faced far greater obstacles.

Although their troops fought strongly and most certainly slowed the offensive in the Argonne, the German High Command knew the war could not be won. On September 28, General Ludendorff lost his self-control. According to some accounts, he fell to the floor, foaming at the mouth.[13] He ranted against the kaiser, the Reichstag, the navy, and the back-stabbing socialists and politicians. His staff closed his door. As Ludendorff already knew, on that same day, Bulgaria, a German ally in the Balkans, had sought an armistice. That meant that the Balkans upon which Germany relied for food and critical high-grade lubricant for airplanes and U-boats could no longer be counted upon. The available supplies would not last long.[14]

With defeat inevitable, Ludendorff feared that the consequence would be a Bolshevik- type revolution which a defeated, demoralized, and perhaps disloyal army would be unwilling or unable to quell.[15] He felt that Germany must seek an armistice. After calming down, that evening he shared his thoughts with the aristocratic General Hindenburg, who had the same concerns. They reasoned that the best way to achieve an armistice that would preserve the army and also deter the feared working-class revolution was to propose a democratization of the government. That way blame would be shared with the back-stabbing socialists. They would invite their socialist critics into more power and propose to accept President Wilson's vague Fourteen Points which had been enunciated in a January 1918 speech as a basis of peace without victory, a better alternative than peace because of defeat.

Their thoughts resonated well with the kaiser, but not with all around him. Chancellor von Hertling resigned because he would not accept the idea of constitutional changes that would lead to democracy. On September 30, 1918, the kaiser appointed Prince Max von Baden, a known liberal, to replace Hertling. This change was part of the plan.

On October 2, the High Command addressed the Reichstag, informing the members that because of the collapse of Bulgaria, German lack of reserves in contrast to the deluge of American soldiers, and the enemy's use of tanks, it was essential to ask for peace now. The following day, Hindenburg issued a statement to Prince Max stating that the High Command insisted upon an immediate peace offer. A note with the proposal of an armistice based on the Fourteen Points was sent to President Wilson on October 5.

Gone were the German visions of the conquest of Europe, domination of the seas, and takeover of the British colonies. Abandoned was the liberation of the Southwest of the United States under the aegis of a Germanized Mexico. Groping for salvage and survival replaced the dreams of glory. Yet the hostilities continued unabated. War became a tool of politicians. Henceforth, the killing would only determine what spoils the victors would be able to exact from the vanquished.

The Little Lead Soldier was unaware of the machinations of those in power and had not written since the Colonel had disengaged from St. Mihiel on September 17. The 61st Infantry had not been required to march immediately to the Argonne. It rested in Manoncourt and Domgermain, near Toul, until its time came. On October 3, the day that Marshal Foch had presented to Pershing the latest plan to place American soldiers under French command because of the chaos that the Tiger had encountered, the Lead Soldier wrote:

3 October 18

Dear Hugh,

My last letter was written from the Potato Cellar just before we marched to the Manoncourt area. That march was different from any other we have made near the front for the regiment marched entire and closed up.

That, in itself, shows how confident our commanders are that the Boche was thoroughly whipped and is too busy protecting himself to take any aggressive action against us.

As we marched back the lines were still banging away at each other and, though it was less lively than it had been for several days, there was still enough fire to keep the "brick" warm but, as we marched further and further from the lines, the boom of the guns became fainter and the shell flashes less vivid. It really seemed rather strange and lonely after the past week.

What a horrible night that was to march! In the afternoon it had cleared up a little but hardly had we started when the very floodgates of the sky seemed to open again and throughout the whole 20 kilometres those poor tired men were drenched. The men were thoroughly fagged from their hard fighting and sleepless nights but they "hung to it" like the men they are and when one dropped it was just because he could not stay on his feet. On the short rest halts, they would lie flat in the wet road and often would have to get aroused to get up and still go on again with the column.

The Colonel sent most of his staff on ahead to rest and be ready for the work of the next morning but he followed his regular custom of riding with the column, stopping several times during the march to let the regiment pass and when the tail of the column was gone by, riding up to the head again. He makes these trips not only for the purpose of judging the condition of the men and for encouraging them and "pepping them up" but also he takes these occasions for expressing his appreciation or complimenting companies or individuals for good work they may have done. Soldiers are just overgrown boys and they are responsive to appreciation by their commanders. Our men will do anything for the Old Man because they know he loves them and appreciates their efforts. His coming back along the column is always the signal for a rise in the spirits of the men and, no matter how tired they may be, his question: "Well men, how is it going?" is sure to be answered: "Fine Sir"—"All right!" "Bully!" Often he will dismount at a halt and chat as freely and easily with the men as though he were one of them and they will be equally frank and friendly with him. Yet there has never been an instance of any man's being impertinent nor disrespectful. The Old Man is boss—there never is any doubt about that—but he and his men are great friends.

On this march, after the events of the past week, he had plenty to say for each company had done something handsome and many of the men had been individually conspicuous:— "Hello, A Company!—They didn't get around that flank, did they?—Bully for you!" "Getting those 16 machine guns was fine, G Company." "Is that H Company? Is Kelly there?—Kelly, your captain told me of your catching those two Boche—you are the real stuff, Kelly!—God Bless You, my boy!" "Hello, Sergeant Hare!—Game was plentiful up on the Kremhilde line— How many did you bag?"

And so it goes through the entire column.

* * *

General Pershing has not asked my opinion nor even told me his plans but I'll bet they are something like what I am writing to you and that tomorrow night we shall be trekking up Verdun way.

Good Night,
Your Soldier

On October 4, Pershing's troops resumed firing. On that same day, the Austro-Hungarian Empire requested an armistice based on President Wilson's Fourteen Points. The following day, which was when General Pershing rebuffed Foch's latest proposal for amalgamation under French command, the Lead Soldier wrote:

5 October 18
Dear Hugh,

My guess is right, so far! We are at Nixeville, ten kilometers southwest of Verdun and, from the looks of things here, and on route here, we have come for business.

* * *

The troops marched so as to arrive there at 4:30 p.m. and they were lined up alongside the truck column. At 5:00 p.m. they "embussed" and at 6:00 p.m. the column started.

What a column! Two hundred camions for our regiment alone!

The other regiments of our division embussed at different points and followed the routes assigned them. Our route was Domgermain—Charmes—Vaucouleurs—Commercy—Bar-le-Duc—Souilly—Nixeville. When you trace that out on your map, you will see there are many other routes leading northward towards Verdun–Argonne. Last night they were all full of truck trains as they have been for several nights past and as they will be for a number of nights more and each of those trucks was carrying twenty Americans to be thrown against that vital Boches position or the material to be used by them in smashing it.

Before the truck train started, the Colonel with the Adjutant, the Lieutenant Colonel, and our French liaison officer, in the Colonel's car, rolled slowly alongside the train and inspected it. When we had passed the head of the train, Hall opened the throttle and we dashed on ahead of the regiment.

We reached Vaucouleurs just at dusk but there was still light enough for us to see where Jeanne d'Arc met the French king.

Soon before midnight we were in Bar-le-Duc. Here we overtook the trucks from another division. It was very difficult to pass this train for the trucks carry only a dim little red pencil

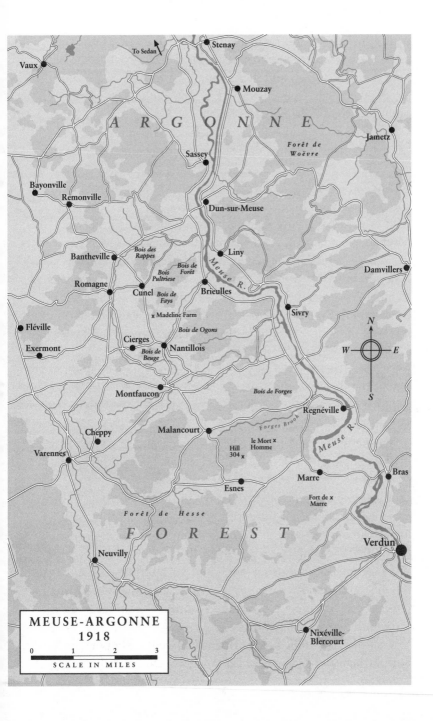

Vaux

To Sedan

Stenay

Mouzay

A R G O N N E

Forêt de
Woëvre

Jametz

Sassey

Bayonville

Remonville

Dun-sur-Meuse

Bois des
Rappes

Bantheville

Liny

Damvillers

Bois de
Forêt

Bois
Pultriese

Meuse R.

Romagne

Cunel

Bois de
Fays

Brieulles

x Madeline Farm

Sivry

Fléville

Bois de Ogons

Exermont

Cierges

Nantillois

Bois de
Beuge

N

W ⊕ E

S

Montfaucon

Bois de Forges

Regnéville

Cheppy

Malancourt

Forges Brook

Meuse R.

Varennes

Hill
304 x

le Mort x
Homme

Bras

Marre

Esnes

Fort de x
Marre

Forêt de Hesse

F O R E S T

Verdun

Neuvilly

Nixéville-
Blercourt

light glowing beneath them. We were miles ahead of our regiment and seemed to be thoroughly blocked in front so the old man decided to stop and have something to eat—"They must have some Bar-le-Duc jelly in Bar-le-Duc" he said as we pulled out of the road in front of the hotel.

Bar-le-Duc was absolutely dark—not a shimmer of light shown anywhere for it is one of the favorite bombing grounds of the Boche.

The dark hallway of the hotel led back into a pretty dining room which was full of American officers.

It is surprising how many Americans one sees everywhere hereabouts and how few Frenchmen. Of course, this is an American sector but, from the men one sees, he might think he was in America. It was the same at Toul where the sky blue uniform was so much less common than the olive drab that the Poilus appear conspicuous. Even the Bar-le-Duc jelly was strangely familiar for it was in the same funny little glasses that it comes in at home.

The reason it is so good and the reason it cannot be successfully imitated is that the currant which grows on the hills about Bar-le-Duc is particularly adapted to making jelly just as the grape of Champagne is to the wine of that name and the grape of Bordeaux is to its wine.

Furthermore, making jelly has been the métier, or specialty of the people of Bar-le-Duc for generations as making champagne has been at Rheims and Epernay.

When we started forward again, the roads were as badly crowded as they were before we stopped—camion company followed camion company and the further north we went the more traffic there was on the road—literally, there were miles after miles of trucks, following one close to another—all rolling steadily on towards where the great American offensive is forming and each carrying forward its 20 units of courage and determination to whip the Boche.

I wonder how much idea Fritz has of what is slipping up on him through the darkness of these nights. Of course he knows that we are moving up but every precaution has been taken to prevent his gaining accurate information as to the size and objective of the movement. That is why we are moving rapidly by trucks—when the sun set, last night, our division was in the Toul area, 70 miles back. When it rose this morning we were close up to Verdun and the trucks were en route back for more troops. So regiments, divisions, and corps are sliding up into the fighting front.

In the morning hours the Colonel's car reached Nixeville, where we found our advanced detachment which came forward yesterday morning to locate camping grounds for the regiment. They had great tales to tell of the great number of troops that had been pouring in up this way and of the immense column of heavy artillery that they had seen.

We had seen some of these ourselves—huge guns which, in the dim starlight, looked like factory smokestacks being hauled along by puffing, snorting tractors.

Nixeville used to be a town. There are still several houses in it with roofs on them.

**

Our column was hours behind us so our party decided to sleep till it came up.

Soon after breakfast, the leading camions of our regiment arrived. Our advance detail had staked out the camp in a beautiful grassy field and, as the companies arrived, they pitched their shelter tents. Regimental headquarters was established in a shack by the roadside in about the center of the camp and the colors were placed in front of it.

We, of course, have no idea how long we were to remain here in this beautiful camp—the first real camp we had been in since we landed in France and much preferable to being kenneled in barns and stables as we usually were.

It has been a beautiful day and a pleasant one and, looking at the regularly laid out camp, one might imagine that we are on a peacetime maneuver were it not for the steady boom of the guns a few miles ahead of us.

At sunset, no intimation had come to us of a move and it seemed probable there would be none tonight so the regimental staff proceeded to get comfortable for the night and the Old Man, having filled a tub with hot water from the radiator of the car, was luxuriating in a hot bath when an aide arrived with orders to be ready to move at 8:00 p.m.

A few minutes later, our supply company arrived after its hard march from Domgermain. The animals were too tired to march on tonight so they had to be bivouacked in the pretty camp we were intending to enjoy.

The battle up front had broken out furiously, which probably accounts for our sudden move—it is 7:30 pm and we move in half an hour—

Good Night,

Your Soldier

On October 6, German prince Max requested that President Wilson "take in hand the restoration of peace," tell the other Allies of the request, and send representatives to negotiate on the basis of the Fourteen Points and other elaborating speeches given by the president. He concluded as follows: "With a view to avoiding further bloodshed, the German Government requests the immediate conclusion of an armistice on land and water and in the air."[16] The same day, the kaiser issued a proclamation to his army informing the soldiers that "I have resolved once more to offer peace to the enemy, but will only extend my hand for an honorable peace." Uncertain of the outcome of the overture, he exhorted: "We must, as hitherto, exert all our strength tirelessly to hold our ground against the onslaught of our enemies."[17]

At the same time, the 61st Infantry was getting ready to actively take on the German forces whose leaders had decided that the war was lost, but, nonetheless, were told to exert all their strength against their enemy. The American soldiers would attack as an American army, not part of a French army. The "invincible obstinacy" of General Pershing had prevailed. The American leaders already knew that they would win the war; the Germans knew that they would lose it.

On October 6, the Lead Soldier wrote:

6 October 18
Dear Hugh,

It is not hard to see that big things are about to happen in this sector and, in fact, all along the western front.

You must not expect me to tell you much about the great operations that are going on nor even much about the operations of our one division of the many divisions that compose this immense force assembling here south of the Argonne Forest.

My promise was to tell you what I see from the dispatch case of one of the regimental commanders and, certainly, you would not expect a lead soldier to write treatises on strategy and tactics to a little boy.

Going back to our own little affair: —at about 7 p.m. last night the battalion commanders assembled in our shed to receive orders which were simple enough—the battalions marched independently, with 5 minutes interval between them—via Dombasle and thence north to the Bois des Esnes which is just south of the famous Hill 304—near Avocourt.

There, our guides, who had been sent ahead, would meet the troops and lead them to the bivouacs in the woods.

While the Colonel was giving the orders and pointing out the route, the unmistakable "whew—whew—whew" of a Boche plane was heard over us and a few seconds later there was the tremendous crash of a bomb—"I think, gentlemen," said the Colonel, "that relieves me of the necessity of impressing you with the advisability of more than ordinary caution as to avions tonight."

At 8 pm the leading battalion marched and the Colonel, with the same officers that came here with him, started forward in the car. The car was a little risky but the horses were too tired to go and it was important that the Colonel should get forward ahead of the troops.

A mile or so after we started, a couple of Boche planes came whewing over the road bombing crossroads where, evidently, they expected troops to be passing.

Fortunately, they were a few minutes ahead of our schedule but several of the bombs lit within a quarter of a mile of us and one lit very close.

You must not think that these bombs are simply overgrown grenades—they are huge pear-shaped steel cans filled, sometimes, with a half-ton or more of high explosives.

One of them will blow a big house to smithereens and will make a hole in the ground big enough to bury an ordinary house in. When one of them explodes, it shakes the whole neighborhood.

* * *

It was raining again now and it was beastly dark in the woods but at every road fork or crossroads our intelligence officer had placed men to direct the columns so we had no difficulty in finding the place where we were to go.

Our regimental headquarters had been located in a very good old French dugout, where we could have a light by which to study those blessed maps at night.

I told you how everything seemed to revolve about those maps at Moyenmoutier—well, it is just the same everywhere else—maps, maps, maps!—Guns are important in war but maps seem to be the real necessity. The intelligence officer had come ahead and located the places for the battalions and had men whom he had brought with him to guide them to them while men from each company waited to lead them.

While this trouble was forestalled, there was another difficulty which was liable to arise from the fact that the four infantry regiments of the division would arrive in these dark woods at about the same time. So the Colonel and the Lieutenant Colonel went back to see that the regiment got on its right road and got its right to the road.

Before daylight, the regiment was in place and had its shelter tents pitched. It was a different camp, however, from the camp we left at Nixeville.

A whole division had to be crowded into these woods and space was very limited. Fallen trees and shell holes break up the surface so there can be no regularity or system in laying out the camp, the ground is boggy so the tents are pitched where there is a dry spot. This was once a fine forest but nearly all the big trees have been cut down or stripped by shellfire so we must depend upon the underbrush for concealment of the shelter tents or camouflage them with green branches and dead brush. The underbrush concealed the tents from a viewpoint on a level with them but it was a big task to cover them all over so they were hid from aerial observation. The next job was to make "hurdles" (wattles of brush) to keep the men out of the mud inside the tents and for the kitchens and supplies. Also, trenches and shell holes had to be prepared to leave cover for the men if Fritz started "tossing things over to us."

So, today was a busy one and it was fortunate that the Boche apparently did not know we were here and overlooked the fine target that Bois des Esnes would be for his "big one."

Ordinarily, the very large guns are not used against troops. Their fire is usually against sensitive points, such as ammunition and ration dumps and important centers of transport, such as cross roads or vulnerable lines of communication. But a nest of troops like this would repay his attentions if he sprinkled it with shell fragments or drenched it with gas. Our headquarters is in a dugout which is remarkable mainly because of what it is made to hold.

It is 8 feet by 20 feet with a pitch of 7 feet.

Along one side of it is a long table which serves as a desk, a place for the beloved maps and a dinner table.

At night, hospital stretchers are put on the floor and others are hung above them to the rafters so there are bunks enough for all the officers who may be permitted to sleep at a time. It is quite different from our handsome luxury at Moyenmoutier and so is the mess. At mealtime the orderlies bring down the food from the supply company kitchen—good wholesome food and plenty of it—on mess pans and coffee in soldier cups and after the regular squabble with the adjutant who has to move his papers, the meal is served.

This is the simple life that all seem happy and satisfied to have even this place to be out of the incessant rain.

We are only about 10 kilometers behind the front lines here and the fight up there is constant. It is particularly lively late in the afternoon and early in the morning when the firing becomes a steady roar.

Our troops up there are edging forward and gaining ground but the Boche is resisting with determination and counter-attacking with fury.

We are in reserve but we know what is ahead of us. It cannot be many days before we move up and leap frog into the row and we are eager for it.

Good Night,
Your Soldier

While the 61st waited impatiently in its makeshift camp, other American troops fought and killed furiously. They also died. Unaffected, the politicians played their cards. On October 8, President Wilson replied through his secretary of state, Robert Lansing, asking for whom Prince Max spoke within the German political structure and whether, in agreeing to the Fourteen Points, the Germans were saying that discussions were necessary only to agree upon the "practical details of their application."[18] Lansing further stated that any good-faith discussions would depend upon the consent of the Central Powers to withdraw their forces immediately from the territories that they had invaded.

On October 10, the Lead Soldier wrote:

10 October 18

Dear Hugh,

I told you that I was not going to write you of strategy and grand tactics nor of the operations of a large unit but I think I shall have to tell you enough of it to give you a general idea of what is going on so you may understand the part we are playing in the big game.

* * *

This great Allied offensive was planned so that each Ally would have his definite part to play. The British are driving eastward through Cambrai, the French northward from Rheims and our part is to strike through the Argonne Forest and along the Meuse River at the railroads between Sedan and Mezieres.

As I wrote you before, breaking those railway lines will not only cut off the main supply of the Boche armies about Rheims but it will also result in the destruction of the hinge on which the Boche armies must swing back from the heavy onslaught of the British and French.

The Boche is, of course, fully aware of these dangers and he will have to weaken his resistance to our allies in order to strengthen his effort against us.

If he weakens against them, they will ruin him and, if he does not reinforce against us, he is lost. Old Fritz is in a bad way at last for our team is playing together—"We'll get him!"—or, as the French say, "On les aura!"

We have that motto now embroidered on a broad blue ribbon tied on the staff of our regimental colors.

While we were reducing the Saint-Mihiel salient, our Allies were driving in their sectors which prevented the Boche sending all the reinforcements there that he might have otherwise sent and as soon as that battle was over we began shifting troops westward for the present drive which will force the Boche to weaken himself in front of the British and French.

This sector has been famous for heavy fighting for, about Verdun, have been some of the hardest fought and bloodiest battles of the war.

The Kronprince's command post for the great battles of Verdun was at Montfaucon (Mountfalcon) where one can still see it, a wonderful dugout, 30 feet underground, equipped with telescopic periscopes so that the "Clown Prince" could watch the battle in safety.

Hills 304 and Mort Homme (Dead Man's Hill), right here at our bivouac are historic spots.

For a year and more, however, this sector has been comparatively inactive. The "Clown Prince," having murdered an army trying to force the French out of Verdun, gave up the attempt and the French apparently saw no hope for driving back the Boche. But recently, the Americans have stirred it up to its old time activity.

* * *

The Colonel and his staff have been buried in their maps for several days and two days ago the regimental and battalion intelligence officers were sent forward to locate the position into which we go when we move forward.

They returned today and this afternoon our leading echelon, the 3rd Battalion, marched. Tomorrow the remainder of the regiment follows.

This afternoon we saw a most wonderful sight—273 American planes went right over us, headed northwards on a bombing expedition.

The squadrons flew in the V formations but they were close together in a huge flock.

This afternoon we received replacements of Saint-Mihiel losses so we shall go in here practically at full strength and we especially needed the 18 lieutenants that we received.

These replacements are mostly men fresh from home—they will make a whirlwind entry—arrive today, do battle tomorrow!

Today we received the official bulletin of Turkey's "blowup"—she is down and out and the Colonel says she will have company before long. He is very confident that this offensive will end the war and I heard him say this afternoon that there would be no fighting after Thanksgiving.

* * *

Good Night,
Your Soldier

Then the 61st Infantry marched into the wasted land. The Lead Soldier wrote:

11 October 18
Dear Hugh,

We marched from Bois des Esnes this morning and today we have an awfully interesting march—a march interesting in its awfulness.

I think I told you how our last campground was knocked down and torn and blown by shells—so is all the rest of the country we came through today, some parts of it worse than others but all bad enough to make it a scene of utter devastation and desolation.

Where villages had been there was sometimes only a trace, a few stones, perhaps, which had not been used by the labor troops for road repair material. Sometimes pieces of battered wall were standing like snags of old teeth on the face of this scarred and pockmarked country that had once been beautiful and smiling.

Where handsome woods had been, only stumps and underbrush remain and, here and there, a dead trunk still standing.

Thousands of shell holes, half filled with water, pitted the surface of oozy yellow mud where had been fields of well cared for crops and green pasture lands.

The very soil itself was turned upside down and is dead to the possibility of agriculture. All over it and under it lie countless unexposed shells which make tilling this land impossible till they are removed. Tangled heaps of barbed wire are everywhere—wrecked trucks, broken down wagons, blown up tanks, abandoned trench machinery cluttered the roadsides and skeletons of horses and occasionally of men lay about in the fields.

In the Philippines one of our generals threatened to make Samar a howling wilderness and, in the Civil War, General Sheridan said he would devastate the Shenandoah Valley so that a crow passing through it would have to carry rations. But this is not a "howling wilderness"—it is too dead to howl and a crow, flying over it, would lose his appetite.

Our route was too exposed to fire and the road was too torn up by shells to be available for wheel transportation so our supply company and the company ration and ammunition cars had to march by a longer though a better route, through Malancourt.

Our column reached Bois de Montfaucon about noon and there our orders directed us to halt till dark.

Meantime, the Colonel had been in touch with the 3rd Battalion which bivouacked near Cuisy last night and moved to Nantillois today and moved up into the line tonight as our leading element. At dark we "formed up, marched" and took our place in the long column of troops which was pushing northward towards the sound of the guns. As we passed over the high hill about a mile north of Bois de Montfaucon, a particularly lively spasm of shelling broke out ahead of us and the sky was vivid with the flash of shells bursting about Nantillois, our destination. Some of our big guns on the hill which we were at the time descending opened up and fairly shook the earth. Poor Yvette was terrified and I got some hard jolting in my dispatch case on her saddle. The Colonel rapped her hard with his crop and called her a "fool" but I cannot see why she was a fool—this is no fight of hers and she has nothing at stake in it. It makes no difference to her who governs Alsace-Lorraine, whether or not the neutrality of Belgium was violated, who owns Kiouchow, whether or not the Berlin–Baghdad railroad is built, nor whether there is freedom on the seas. She did, however, have horse sense enough to realize that her head was in momentary danger of being knocked off by a Boche shell and she was simply protesting in her equine way.

Soon after passing Montfaucon or, rather, what used to be Montfaucon—it is now only a collection of stone heaps and a sign board, we were held up a long time waiting for the Boche to get through with strafing the road between there and Nantillois. Then we hurried forward before he turned his guns on us again.

He did catch our column with one or two shells but our casualties were nothing like what we might have expected.

Before arriving at Nantillois, the Colonel and the adjutant galloped ahead to the PC of the commander of the brigade we were to relieve and, from him received the orders for relieving some of his troops on the line. When the column reached Nantillois, he met it and gave the majors their instructions and, returning to the brigade PC, received further orders which are to attack in the morning.

That PC is a remarkable place—it is a cellar, or crypt of a once handsome church. The church is completely battered down but the debris of its walls make a thick pile on its strong arch supported floor and the crypt beneath it is, therefore, a fairly safe bombproof. But, is it not a queer place for a command post? Under the flagstones of its floor are buried the dead—over them, live men, who may be snuffed out at any moment, study maps and making plans for killing other men.

By the time the Colonel came out the regiment had passed on its way into the line—each battalion going to its assigned position.

The 3rd Battalion is in Bois de Fay, the 2nd Battalion supporting it, and the 1st Battalion is between Bois de Malmont and Bois de Foray. The headquarters company is in Bois de Ogons but as detachments of 37s, Signal, and Pioneers out with the battalions.

Coming out of the brigade PC, the Colonel called to the staff to "Mount Up" and directed that an extra horse be turned over to the guide who was to take us to Bois de Ogon:—"But, sir, you are not going there mounted, are you?" protested the guard—"Certainly I am," replied the Old Man. "The Boche is showing pretty regular, sir"—"Don't you suppose I know that?—I'm not blind or deaf! Mount up and lead out!"

"I think it would be safer for you on foot," said a staff officer, as we emerged from behind the ruins—"That's where you are mistaken, my boy," replied the Colonel. "We're bigger targets on horsebacks but we aren't exposed so long—Trot out!"

Away we went at a swinging trot. The staff were accustomed to tricks like this from the Colonel and most of them believed he was right but the guard, who seemed to be a poor horseman, as well as a poor mathematician, was not convinced and he was uncertain in his head as well as in his seat.

Just as we passed out of town—"Blooey!—Wow!" A big one burst among the ruins 100 yards behind us and a shower of stones landed in the road where we had just passed. "Now! Will you believe me?" laughed the Colonel—"If we had been walking, we should have been about back there and we would be flying now."

The night was fairly light and the road was visible enough for the horses to avoid shell holes. Fortunately, Fritz was strafing elsewhere. We could see the flash of his shells but none of them landed very close to us and we arrived at our PC safely.

There was no place there for the horses and a casual look showed that they would be killed if kept there so the Colonel ordered them back to the supply company near Septsarges. Then he and his staff went into the PC where were the colonel and staff of the regiment we were to relieve.

They had had several days of hard fighting and were pretty well tired out and they were unmistakably glad to see us.

They had a lot of severe gassing so their colonel and his adjutant could hardly see nor speak.

For two hours the old man and the other colonel have been studying maps together and each of our staff officers has been busily going over his work with a corresponding outgoing staff officer. It sounds like a sewing circle in here.

Good Night,
Your Soldier

Perhaps St. Mihiel could be described properly by some as a cakewalk. Now, it really was time for the 61st to "do." On October 12, the Lead Soldier wrote:

12 October 18

Dear Hugh,

This is the real thing now: The world has probably never before seen such desperate fighting!

Our army is determined to drive the Boche back and open the way to the final objective and the Boche, knowing full well what that would mean to him, is equally determined to prevent it.

Our Allies are continuing their magnificent offensives and are sweeping the Boche back on the Western Front and we are gaining ground and morale every day.

The Boche is trying to withdraw from them and is swinging his army back on the pivot in front of us.

The destruction of that pivot will mean his certain defeat and, cost what it may, our commanders are bent upon destroying it.

This seems to be the opportunity for the Allies to push in and bring on the decision—the sparring stages of this contest have passed—the time has come for infighting and a knockout. If we smash this hinge which the Boche army is trying to swing back on, there can be but one result—the end of the war.

Our army, corps, division, brigade and regimental commanders have all been made to understand this and are throwing their commands against the Boche position with determination to pay the price but to get the results.

From the commander-in-chief down to the privates, all realize that "pour faire une omelette, il faut casser des oeufs." And, however costly in lives this policy may be now, it will later save life for, even though we suffer excessive casualties this autumn, we will not equal the losses we would incur by undergoing a severe winter in the trenches followed by a spring drive against a re-organized Boche.

We have Fritz going now and we must force him to the ropes.

The Boche is not demoralized but victory has lately deserted his colors and while we have him going backwards, we must crowd him hard to get him on the run.

Our commanders realize all this no more than do our rank and file whose spirit, courage, and determination are simply wonderful. Cold, fatigue, danger—nothing daunts them nor lessens their zeal. Beat them back and punish them cruelly as you may, the Boche has them to meet again renewing their attacks with the same élan of fresh troops—They throw themselves upon him with the abandon of the Dervish but not in the Dervish's delirium of emotion for theirs is not the courage of fanaticism but of dogged Anglo-Saxon determination to win in the cause which they all understand.

Oh—Hukins, they are too splendid to describe. America can be proud of these hero sons of hers in the ranks—these fresh, clean, healthy boys who, protected only by woolen coats, defy steel fragments and take machine guns with their rifle butts.

The Boche is fast learning what an aggressive, vicious fighter this good-natured generous American boy can be and he is unmistakably afraid of him in single combat on equal terms. Probably this fear counts for the deep hatred he has for the American soldier which hatred is reciprocated by our men who detest and loathe the dishonorable and brutal characteristics of the Boche.

From childhood, our boys are taught to play fair in their games and to fight fair in their fights, to respect an honest adversary and to take no mean advantage of him. Their contempt is, therefore, unbounded for this enemy for whom no deceit is too low and no trick too foul and no atrocity too degrading.

This mutual hatred has robbed this war of all chivalry and leaves it simply the most cold-blooded and scientific butchery in history.

But I must get back to my story—I told you that we had orders to attack at daylight. This was but our part in the general push all along our front to secure the important, tactical and strategic points. It is also another turn of the grindstone that is wearing down the Boche.

The task of our regiment was a hard one because the attack must follow a weary night of making relief and was to be made over ground that we had not reconnoitered, nor even seen and against an enemy whose position and strength we knew only from reports that were probably none too accurate.

Throughout the relief, the Boche kept up a murderous bombardment of the front line, the supports, and the reserves and the command post, using high explosives and gas till the wood reeked with mustard phosgene. Frequently he supplemented his vicious bombardment with rafaels [crescendo waves] of machine gun fire and his armed men had only the shelter of shell holes or hasty entrenchments, our casualties were heavy.

You remember how, at Saint-Mihiel, every detail of the assault was planned ahead and how the battalion commanders were assembled for explanation and discussion. Also how the artillery prepared the way for the infantry advance and how it rolled an accompanying barrage ahead to mash down Boche opposition.

Here, the majors could not be assembled because they were not only making relief but were also directing the fight on the line. Their orders had to be sent to them on pages from the field notebook and explanations given in sketches on battle maps.

That is another map! When troops are going into action, hundreds of "battle maps" are distributed to the organization commanders—these are sheets, about 8 inches by 16 inches, showing a section of country, about 2 kilometers by 4 kilometers, where combat is likely to occur. On the reverse side of the sheet is space for explanations and notes. All the officers going in last night had these battle maps on which they could sketch information they might acquire.

When the Colonel ordered the assault this morning, he sent to the battalion commanders maps on which were sketched, in color pencil, our position and the Boche position and lines indicating the direction and limits for the attack.

The battalion commanders, having studied out the details, gave their orders in the same way.

Staff officers were sent out to the battalions with the orders and maps for the attack and while they were doing this, the Colonel was getting information and instruction from the colonel he was relieving.

To still further embarrass matters, the Boche put over several large doses of gas which suspended things while our masks were on.

Altogether, it was "nuit blanche" but, before daylight, the relief was made and our battalions were in position and the first battalion, crouched in shell holes, awaited the signal to "go over."

In this attack, we could expect little artillery support and no accompanying barrage. Our lines were too irregular and too close to the Boche lines to justify the risk of firing on the Boche from the artillery's position in the rear. The woods were so dense and the ground so broken that it was next to impossible to tell where the lines were. It was just a plain case of infantry having to go in and fight it out.

At the crack of dawn, the 1st Battalion, supported by the 2nd Battalion with the 3rd Battalion in reserve, "took off" from its line 300 yards north of the Brieulles–Cunel road and attacked straight north.

There was no yelling nor cheering as they sprang from the shell holes and pressed steadily forward. There was no need to advertise their coming to the Boche and every second of unresisted advance meant lives saved. But the Boche was ever watchful as always and our lines had gone but a few yards when up went parachute rockets hanging over it the dazzling white lights that showed everything as by day "whiiiiir"! went the machine guns along the Boche line—"tac, tac, tac"!, the automatics—and then the roar of rifle fire!

We were too close in on them for them to use their artillery on our advancing line but they opened up a searching fire for our supports and reserves and pounded the woods mercilessly.

Our line was crossing an open strip between the take off and the Boche line. To stop would be folly, to retreat was not to be thought of—it quickened its pace and then took up the double, firing not a shot but closing with gun butt and bayonet, clubbing and prodding the Boche from his trenches and that, by the way, is the fighting most to the American taste and the kind in which he most excels—he seems to regard it as more sportsmanlike than the use of long range weapons.

On the other hand, Fritz does not like that kind of fighting at all and he is quick to "hands up" and yell "Kamarade" when he is cornered for a bayonet fight.

Our objective, the northern edge of the Bois de Foret was taken and with it a number of prisoners and machine guns.

Because of the difficulty of moving these and of the danger that they might be retaken, machine guns were destroyed except a few which could be immediately used against the enemy. Immediately, the line began "digging in" for cover from the shelling which we knew would follow and which did come as soon as the Boche line had cleared itself. Our line might have followed the Boche for a further advance but that would have put us in an untenable position and it would not have been playing in the team as we were trying to do.

So it was that our first night here was spent and it was a strenuous night and morning. We had lost heavily, including a number of officers among them the gallant little major who led the assault, but we have made one more step forward in the "big push" and the troops on our right and left have stepped forward with us.

All forenoon the Boche continued his bombardment with unceasing fury. Losses piled up in all the battalions, especially in the first battalion which was hanging onto its exposed forward position. This phase of the fight was far more trying than had been the assault. In the attack, the men had the stimulus of action and the élan of aggression. Now they could only burrow into the ground to escape the rain of shell fragments and shrapnel balls with no chance to strike back.

Our artillery tried to counter on the Boche batteries but had little effect on them for their location was not known and, they, knowing exactly our lines, continued pounding us. About noon, a Boche avion circled over our regimental PC and, having evidently located it, flew away towards the north. A few minutes later, we received an awful strafing. Trees all around us were cut down and a little village on the crest above us was utterly demolished. Our dugout was hit by hundreds of fragments, but, by a miracle, it escaped a direct hit which would have finished it for it was only a trench covered with corrugated iron topped with about three feet of dirt. It is rain proof but by no means proof against even the smallest shells.

When the tornado had passed, our wireless was wrecked, telegraph and telephone communication was cut and all visual apparatus was out of commission and we were reduced to runner relays.

To paralyze the regimental command post or to cut off its communication with the battalions, had, of course, been the purpose of this heavy shelling.

This effort to isolate the regimental PC and numerous other incidents of the day convinced the Colonel that there was going to be a strong counter attack from the Boche so he directed the major of the 3rd Battalion to reinforce the 1st Battalion with two of his companies. Hardly had this been done when, following another intense bombardment, a line of Boche infantry, supported by tanks, came forward.

They were magnificent to see as they came on in perfect wave formation and our groups in the line of surveillance had to fall back before them. They were not more than 200 meters away when our line and all of our machine guns cut loose at them and the rifle grenadiers let fly with their "VB" and phosphorus grenades.

The Boche line staggered, wavered and stopped but it held to its ground and, in the hot fight that ensued, neither side was gaining very decided advantage but their tanks were a power for them.

Breathless runners came to the PC with reports and battle maps and urgent appeals for artillery help against the tanks. Runners were started back to the artillery asking for a barrage but it was a mere chance that any one of them would be received in time for the artillery fire to be of service.

The Colonel stood outside the PC, receiving and sending messages and looking anxiously towards the line where our men were holding.

"What a chance!" he exclaimed—"If I could only get the artillery!" And, at that moment, the signal officer ran up and reported—"We have our wire repaired!—Quick Colonel before it is broken again!" The Colonel grabbed the instrument from the signal officer—"Give me Solomon—Quick!"—"This is Soakem, Solomon!—A barrage on our SOS line and roll it north—Hurry. It's our chance—there are tanks!"

Three minutes later the phone buzzed—"The batteries have fired sir,!" came the joyous tidings and almost simultaneously there was a screaming, screeching, and whizzing as the shells went over us—then the rip and crash of the shells burst in front of our line—the barrage had landed right in front of the Boche line and began to creep forward sweeping them back before it—leaving behind as markers a line of motionless field gray forms to show where the Boche line had been.

"Great!" said the Old Man as he laid aside the receiver.

The Boche counter attack had absolutely failed and he had paid a heavy price for the effort. We re-occupied our line of surveillance and the Boche reopened his relentless shelling and, as though he realized that the nerve center of the regiment was still functioning, he evidently assigned several guns to pound our PC.

It is midnight—there will be no sleep here tonight but happy dreams to you.

Your Soldier

On that same day, October 12, 1918, German chancellor Prince Max replied to the American secretary of state reiterating that Germany accepted the Fourteen Points as the foundation of a permanent peace and, answering the American inquiry, stated that the purpose of discussions now "would be only to agree upon the practical details of the application of these terms."[19] The chancellor also stated that he assumed that the other Allied governments also took the position of the United States and followed with: "The German Government in accordance with the Austro-Hungarian Government, for the purpose of bringing about an armistice, declares itself ready to comply with the proposition of the President with regard to evacuation." The note concluded with the assurance that the chancellor was speaking in the name of the people and the government, supported by the will of the great majority of the Reichstag. Right then the war should have been over, but it was not.

The president had to think about it. The following day, while Wilson was mulling the German reply, it was business as usual in the Argonne. The Lead Soldier wrote:

13 Oct 18
Dear Hugh,

It was a bleary eyed bunch which the daylight shone in upon when the cover of the entrance was pulled back to let fresh air into the foul dugout.

Not much light can get into the dugout so candles have to burn day and night. At night, the one source of ventilation is closed so the light may not show outside so you can imagine how horrible the place becomes.

There, on one side of the table, this morning, sat the Colonel, his hand on the telephone, staring at the map—I should think he would know every line of it by now!

Opposite him, his head on the table, sat the Adjutant—his field order book and pencil ready beside him. Other members of the staff sat about on the floor catching a few minutes of sleep where they leaned wearily against the wall during this lull in the fight when nothing was going on but a desultory shelling.

The telegraph operator nodded over his instrument which was silent for the first time in hours.

In the trench, by the entrance, a dozen runners were waiting for the calls that sent them on their perilous missions.

The second night of continuous fighting was ended and the second day was commencing.

Reilley comes in and makes coffee in a big can over a solid alcohol lamp and fishes out of a gunny sack some hard biscuit, "Bully Beef" and a can of blackberry jam.

"Wake up!" Shouts the Old Man—"It's breakfast time!" And, as a shell whistles overhead, he adds "the birds are singing welcome to the morn." They all fall to eating while they have the chance—laughing and joking as though there were no possibility that the next bird may light on our roof and scatter their fragments in the surrounding trees.

* * *

The Colonel and the Lieutenant Colonel went outside and stood for a while talking in low tones after which the Lieutenant Colonel went off with several runners toward Bois de Foret and the Colonel sat on top of the dugout awaiting the result of his request on the artillery.

In about 5 minutes it came—a storm of high explosive shells and gas shells and broke like a thundercloud on the spot where Colonel had made the X on the map. "I guess that will hold them for a while," he remarked, smiling at the Adjutant who had joined him.

"Good morning greetings to Fritz," replied the Adjutant. "I don't believe he overslept last night, anyway."

If the Boche had any intention of making an effort from that point, he abandoned it and, for the remainder of the forenoon, his infantry contented itself with sniping and with several brisk little skirmishes along the line.

His artillery, however, grew more active and all the morning our regiment had to grind its teeth and hold on in the face of a terrific bombardment to which we could not retaliate and which, not withstanding our hasty entrenchments, caused us heavy losses.

They got in several times on our command posts and we lost two of our staff officers that day but the regiment held hard to its gains and when the leading elements of the regiment that came to relieve us arrived, we were prepared to turn over to them all that we had been sent to take.

During the day, the new regiment filtered into the position and we began filtering out and back towards Nantillois where the battalions were to assemble and form for an attack tomorrow morning.

The withdrawal from our lines was very difficult for the Boche not only kept up an incessant shelling of the position but also he rolled several barrages across the valley through which we had to pass en route to our assembly point.

It was well past midnight when the regiment was back to the place of formation where the weary men dropped in the muddy field and slept, unmindful of rain and shells.

In the meantime, the Colonel and some of his staff had been to brigade headquarters and had received the directions for tomorrow's attack. They returned about midnight to this little shelter in Bois de Beuge to work out the details of the orders which were then hurried to the battalion commanders.

About 2:00 a.m. the Old Man threw himself onto a hospital stretcher and asked to be called in an hour. Just as he did so, the Lieutenant commanding the Stokes Mortar Platoon came in— "Hello! Stokes," said the Colonel, "you covered yourself with glory yesterday and today—those tubes of yours did great work!—I am proud of you and your men!"

This Lieutenant is a big handsome fellow with a boyish face that is always smiling. The Colonel is very fond of him and put him in command of the Stokes platoon because he is absolutely loyal, dependable, intelligent, and courageous. When he is given a job to do, nothing but impossibility can stop him.

He was a guard on the Yale football team a few years ago and he plays this game as he played that.

You remember his barrage at Mère Henry and his gas shelling of the thicket La Forain. At Saint-Mihiel and here he has done quite as well.

He went over to the corner where the Colonel lay and put a blanket over him—"You'll catch cold, Colonel," he said—"and we can't have you sick tomorrow."

He hung around with something apparently on his mind— "What's the matter, Stokes—What's on your mind?" demanded the Colonel. "Oh! Sir," replied Stokes, with one of his boyish smiles, "the orders for tomorrow hold my platoon in rear." "Yes," replied the Colonel—"your outfit could not keep up in the advance—the mud, rough ground, woods—but I'll call you up when there is use for you."

Stokes still hesitated and the Old Man said: "Out with it Stokes—what do you want?"—"Well, sir—may I leave the platoon with the sergeant till you want us and may I go forward with K Company?—You know it lost all its officers today and it's my old company." "You bet you may, my boy!" replied the Colonel—"Go to it!—Take the company—I'm going to see that you are its captain when this fight is over!"

Out went Stokes, beaming with joy, and I advise Fritz to keep out of K Company's way today.

The Colonel is getting his nap—it's nearly 3 o'clock—he'll have things stirring soon.

Good night

Your Soldier

THIRTEEN

DEBACLE

ON OCTOBER 14, 1918, PRESIDENT WILSON REPLIED TO Prince Max that the conditions of an armistice must be left to the judgment and advice of the military advisors and must provide guarantees of the present military supremacy of the United States and its Allies.[1] On that same day the Lead Soldier wrote:

14 Oct 18
Dear Hugh,

Dawn had to push its way through mist and rain again on this third day of our fighting here.

The men awoke cold and stiff on their mud beds and ready and eager for the fray. They realize that we have the Boche going and they are anxious to keep on pushing him.

We left our place in Bois de Beuge soon after daylight and established the regimental PC near the Nantillois–Cunel road, about half a kilometer north of Nantillois.

When we arrived there, the battalions were moving into their "take off" positions and, passing along the leading battalion, the Colonel was speaking to the men and asking them how they felt, and, generally letting them see that he appreciated their work and knew their hardships.

They all looked rather miserable—wet, cold, and muddy but they smiled back cheerfully at the Colonel and showed that their spirit was still in them.

"You look pretty cold, my man" he said to one youngster—"Yes sir—I can't seem to remember when I was dry or warm," the soldier replied with a laugh. "Don't you suppose, sir we're ever going to get better weather than this?"

"I hope not" replied the Colonel, "for this is harder on the Boche than it is on us—we are better fed and better clothed than he is!"—"That's right!" replied the soldier—"I hadn't thought of it that way! & Let it rain!"

"We'll warm Fritz today!" shouted another man—"We will that!" replied the Colonel, passing on down the line.

Our Brigade was formed 300 meters in rear of the other Brigade of the Division which led off on this attack—we were to leap-frog them later.

We formed with the 2nd and 3rd Battalions in line on the ridge 200 meters north of the Cierges–Nantillois road—all companies in line of platoons in four waves.

The 1st Battalion was in support, 300 meters in rear of the 3rd Battalion, the right battalion on the line.

It had not been so quiet hereabouts for several days as it was for an hour or two preceding the H Hour of this attack.

Our guns were waiting the time for opening the preparation and counter-battery fire and for dropping the accompanying barrage, all of which were, in this case, to be simultaneous.

The Boche seemed to be taking a long breath and was getting ready for us.

It was like two prize fighters resting between rounds—awaiting the bell.

At the H Hour, the signal came with the roar of hundreds of big iron throats behind our lines—They seemed to cheer their champion into the fight while hundreds from the other side shouted defiance at him. The boom of guns, the rush of projectiles and the crash of shells blended into one mighty din as the storm of battle swept on.

Onward the assault pressed, driving back the Boche lines till they met the stiffer resistance in the trenches south of Cunel.

Meantime, our regiment, following close behind, was ready to leap-frog the advance troops when they had spent their strength.

From the take-off, our regimental headquarters moved along the Nantillois–Cunel road between our leading battalions and established a temporary PC at Ferme Madeleine.

Up to here, our casualties had been mainly from shells and in the valley at Ferme Madeleine the shelling was terrific. It seemed that one could not look at any spot of ground for a minute before he saw it spouted into the air by a bursting shell.

Our forward lines had pushed to the top of the wooded hill north of Ferme Madeleine where the Boche was meeting them with machine gun and rifle fire now while he evidently used the bulk of his artillery to prevent the passage of the following lines through the valley in their rear.

Our regiment pressed steadily on, following the leading regiment into the Bois Cunel and then, leap-frogging it, swept down the open slope and over the Boche trenches.

On, we swept, breaking and driving back the Boche lines on the Cunel–Romagne road, our PC following along and establishing in a road ditch about 300 meters south of Cunel.

Soon before noon, after a desperate fight, the 2nd and 3rd Battalions held a line parallel to the Romagne–Cunel road and a quarter of a mile north of it and the supporting battalion was in the woods just north of Cunel.

Here orders were received to cease advancing and to hold so the battalions were ordered to "dig in."

Throughout the afternoon, the Boche kept up a heavy shelling of our position and added considerably to our already heavy casualties but it did not weaken our determination to hold what we had and to take more when we were authorized to do it.

Several attempts to counter-attack were beaten back and night came on with our lines along the entire American front resting where the Boche had been that morning.

What a day it has been! And what a glorious day, in spite of our losses! What heroes these men are! How they've fought! They are like tigers!

And, after it all, they are lying out there in the mud—cold, wet and hungry but game and ready for it all over again!

Their fighting blood is up good now and the Boche has a further reckoning to make with them for not only is their purpose to whip the Boche strengthened but also they want revenge and more revenge for the men and officers we have lost today.

K Company, for example, will make him pay dearly for their commander—"Stokes." He was killed this morning right at the regimental PC at Ferme Madeleine, and, as he lay there where he fell, the boyish smile still on his face, I heard the Colonel mutter: "God bless you, my boy—there are not enough Boche in Germany to pay for you—On les aura!"—And the entire regiment would say "Amen."

About dusk the Intelligence Officer, hunting a place where we could have a light at night, located a Boche dugout near where we were in the ditch by the roadside.

So, we moved in here. The pioneers have thrown up a little parapet to cover the entrance which, of course, faces the wrong way and the signal platoon has connected us up with battalions and Brigade headquarters.

Candles are lighted, the maps are spread, and all starts off for another sleepless night—Our fourth in this battle.

The Boche shelling continues—It probably will continue. We should be very lonely without it. But we've got Fritz going!

Good night

Your Soldier

15 Oct 18

Dear Hugh,

I wonder if you realize what a severe test yesterday was! The physical exertion required of the men was, in itself, heavy and added to that the nervous tension made it a hard strain.

The battalions had spent the night before struggling through the mud in rain and darkness to be in position for this attack and to extricate themselves from the woods where for two days and two nights they had been fighting continuously.

The men had been shelled, gassed, and raked by machine guns constantly: and undergone several intense bombardments; and made a difficult though successful attack; and had resisted a fierce counter-attack. They had dug trenches, moved, and dug again.

All this time they had been without shelter, exposed to a cold driving rain and without warm food—They were wet, chilled, and tired when called upon for even greater efforts but they responded with the energy and spirit of fresh troops.

Neither the hardships to which the individuals had been subjected nor the disorganization, consequent to having started this attack before there had been time to re-organize after the Bois de Foret fight deterred them nor lessened their will and determination to "bust through and run over" the Boche opposition and they did this in spite of a stubborn and courageous defense which inflicted cruel losses upon them.

Soon after midnight, the Colonel was called to Brigade Headquarters for conference and he and the Intelligence Officer, putting on their helmets, floundered out in the mud to the road leading back to Ferme Madeleine.

The night was so dark that one could not see his hand before him except when the flash of bursting Boche shells vividly lighted the way and showed not only the road and the shell holes in it but also the debris and the carnage of battle that lay along it.

It seemed more than an even chance that they would never reach the Brigade PC and a still less of a chance that they would return but, in about two hours, they came back with orders to make another attack today.

We were to drive ahead and clear the western half of Bois Pultriere and Bois des Rappes, connecting with the other regiment of our brigade on our right, while our other brigade advanced on our left.

* * *

Before daylight, the first battalion took up its attack formation on a generally East–West line extending from a point about 300 meters north of Cunel to the Cunel–Bantheville road and connecting on its right and left with the leading battalions of other regiments.

The 3rd Battalion formed in rear of the 1st and the 2nd in rear of the 3rd. You can see that the formation was similar to that of yesterday but it was even deeper and more compact and was intended to ram in and break through the Boche defense, cost what it might—the omelette had to be made and we had to break eggs.

But these were not the full battalions which attacked in Bois de Foret, nor the big battalions that attacked here yesterday for casualties and exhaustion had reduced them to less than one-third of their former strength.

The spirit and courage of the men was, however, undiminished and determination showed in their faces as they crouched in the shell holes awaiting the H hour while the earth rocked and reeled with the thunder of our preparation fire and the Boche counter-preparation.

H hour arrived!—Our accompanying barrage fell and crept forward!—"Up and over!"—With clenched teeth and set faces, the waves scrambled from the shell holes and they were off!

The Boche counter-barrage dropped!—His machine guns hissed!—The rasping rattle of his infantry fire joined in the chorus!

The dense woods were an inferno of shrieking, screaming, crashing shells! Big trees were uprooted and cut down and the air was full of their flying branches. The very atmosphere seemed hot from the rush of projectiles! But through it all pressed those khaki lines, on, on, on, leaving their trails of writhing and motionless forms but unhesitating, and, dashing through the shower of grenades, they leaped with their gleaming bayonets upon the Boche trenches and on, on, on, the successive waves leap-frogged till the position was ours!

On account of the difficulty of locating our lines in the thick woods, our accompanying barrage had to be dropped well ahead of us and this left a strip along the northern edge of Bois de Pultriere and the southern edge of Bois des Rappes unscathed by our shells.

This strip was infested with machine gun nests which had to be cleaned out by the infantry.

Each of these presented its own difficult little problem for, however we may hate the Boche, we must give him credit for being a courageous hard fighter.

Nothing could be handsomer than the way his machine gunners stuck to their guns today till prodded away from them with the cold steel or burned to death at them with phosphorus grenades.

Our men, working around in rear of a nest, and taking it at great cost would invariably find themselves under fire of more nests in the rear and still more further back.

In some cases the Boche had camouflaged his machine guns in dugouts which allowed our lines to pass and then he came out of his hole and fired into our backs.

They were like hornets everywhere with fatal stings.

It was noon when Bois Pultriere was finally ours and then there remained the task of forcing the crossing of the open strip between that and the Bois des Rappes and of clearing out those woods which were known to be even more strongly held than were the Pultriere woods.

From the western edge of Bois des Rappes which was thickly studded with machine guns, the Boche could crossfire on the advance of our other brigade which was thus held up till we could clear the woods which we therefore had to do at all costs.

The Boche's supply of machine guns seemed to be inexhaustible—all the morning we had been capturing and destroying them only to find more in our front. The gunners who were not killed or captured kept falling back to other guns ready in their rear with which they could open up afresh.

As this proceeding bid fair to continue indefinitely, the solution of the problem was to prevent the retirement of the gunners.

In order to place a barrier between them and to smash the nests along the western edge of the woods, a barrage was dropped along the northern and western edge of the Bois des Rappes.

Our regiment reformed and drove forward again, forcing the crossing of the clearing and entering Bois des Rappes where fighting like that of this morning was repeated with perhaps even greater fury.

When a battalion or a company was checked, the one in its rear passed through it and took over the fight while it re-formed for another leap-frog when its turn came. So they went on leap-frogging through the forest till between 3 pm and 4 pm, the remnants of the 2nd Battalion had gained the northern edge of the woods and parts of the 1st and 3rd Battalions held its western edge.

Our losses had been exceedingly heavy, especially among officers and non-commissioned officers. The 1st and 3rd Battalions had lost their commanders and, in the regiment, there remained an average of less than one officer per company of the seven each had had when we entered this battle.

So rapidly had the company, platoon, and squad leaders been bowled over that the men did not know who were their commanders and the regular succession of command was often replaced by the assumption of authority by some self-reliant fellow who, seeing the necessity for a leader rose to the emergency, formed groups of the scattered men and led them on.

As a result of the stiff resistance in the woods, the heavy shelling, the confusion of forest fighting and the frequent passing of organizations through one another; units were badly mixed and the difficult task of re-organizing had to be undertaken after our objective was gained.

Also it had become necessary for the 2nd Battalion, along the northern edge of the woods, to spread out to the right to cover some of the space which should have been held by another regiment. Therefore, there was no definite organization to the line which was rather a chain of small groups trying to maintain touch with each other.

The same condition was largely so along the western edge of the woods as well.

With the few officers that remained with the decimated companies, the old organization was impossible. The Colonel therefore ordered the one captain who remained in the northern line to apportion his groups among his few remaining officers and to handle them as one company.

Those on the western edge were similarly handled and the remainder of the regiment was organized into a battalion of two small companies for a support.

You see, our three big battalions had been reduced to four small companies and we had our objective and the Bois des Rappes was ours.

It would have been a great chance for the Boche to counterattack us while we were restoring order to our shattered lines but he was worse broken than we were and he could not attack.

Since sunset there has been no aggressive movement by the infantry on either side though the artillery of both sides continues its pounding.

It is midnight now. The Colonel is just back from another trip to the Brigade PC where he was called for another conference. We have established ourselves in the PC where we were last night but there is a better ventilation in it now for, about a hour ago, a "whiz bang" (that's what they call an Austrian 88 cm) took off piece of the top.

Good night

Your Soldier

On October 6, 1918, the Germans had requested an armistice, but the killing had continued and even increased. It was as if all leaders agreed with British general Haig that "We lament too much over death."

For all too many, the attack in Meuse-Argonne became the charge into the Valley of Death, made famous in Tennyson's poem "The Charge of the Light Brigade." Lives were squandered in October and November 1918 on a cause already lost by the Germans and already won by the Allies. Killing mandated by inept leaders and inflicted in pursuit of honor are the similar themes. So is the heroism. I quote again from the last letter:

H hour arrived!—Our accompanying barrage fell and crept forward!—"Up and over!"—With clenched teeth and set faces, the waves scrambled from the shell holes and they were off!

The Boche counter-barrage dropped!—His machine guns hissed!—The rasping rattle of his infantry fire joined in the chorus!

The dense woods were an inferno of shrieking, screaming, crashing shells! Big trees were uprooted and cut down and the air was full of their flying branches. The very atmosphere seemed hot from the rush of projectiles! But through it all pressed those khaki lines, on, on, on, leaving their trails of writhing and motionless forms but unhesitating, and, dashing through the shower of grenades, they leaped with their gleaming bayonets upon the Boche trenches and on, on, on, the successive waves leap-frogged till the position was ours!

The Lead Soldier next wrote:

16 Oct 18
Dear Hugh,
All last night and today the Boche has kept up the same savage shelling and our casualties continue to mount but he has not the slightest chance of driving us out of the positions we have paid so heavily for.

The Colonel has repeatedly asked for counter-battery work from our artillery but, though it has made its utmost endeavor, it has not been able to put the Boche guns out of action or to slacken their fire to any great extent.

The trouble is that we cannot locate the Boche guns. One of their batteries seems to have selected our PC as the object of its special attentions. A plane located us this morning and since then, the Boche guns have scored two direct hits on the dugout and have churned up the surrounding ground into a regular mud pudding.

Our intelligence officer was busy all day trying to locate the Boche batteries. He has gotten the direction of some of their guns by taking compass bearings of shell furrows but he has not been able to find a fuse-plug with a range set on it.

Fritz has been particularly lavish with his gas shells today and the woods reek of phosgene and yperite.

We have had heavy doses of it here too in our PC and have to wear masks a good part of the day, which seriously interferes with the work. There have been heavy gas casualties today as every day of this battle, especially among the wounded who are not able to adjust their masks.

We have had no more infantry attacks here by either side. The Boche is evidently too crippled to counter-attack and our orders are "to hold." Our play was to carry the ball through the Bois des Rappes and, having done that, we now await the next signal from the team captain.

But, though neither side has attacked, fighting has been continuous and vicious all day between the lines in place.

Along some parts of the American front there is great activity today but, here, the antagonists are two prizefighters in a clench—pushing back and forth and jabbing when they get an arm free.

Both are fatigued and weakened from loss of blood but our man is still steady on his feet and the other fellow is groggy. Our fellow's jabs have steam behind them and the other fellow's are quite feeble.

If the Boche has lost his punch here, he has not got it anywhere for he has been shifting his best troops here to stop our thrust at his pivot.

In doing this, he must have had to weaken his resistance to our allies and the British have him going backwards in a rout while the French are forcing him out in their sector.

The prisoners we captured today were from the first Prussian guards, the best Boche troops.

We had a lot of them in the PC today and the change in them is very noticeable. They were not the old-time, arrogant, defiant Boche. The thrashings they have recently had have evidently tamed them considerably and have set them thinking about what they are up against.

Until recently, it had been perfectly inconceivable to them that any troops could stand against them and it had been preposterous to think that the "Fatherland" could be defeated. Now, they are by no means so sure about it.

It is now a question of only a few days before the Boche must break in our front and when he does, it will be all over with him.

Before you receive this letter, he will be beaten to his knees and ready to accept any terms the Allies see fit to give him.

He will receive no pity from the world for he deserves none. He has never been fair to others.

The best we can say for the Boche is that he is good fighter and a splendid soldier but, withal, a cruel, treacherous brute that must be caged.

Having completed the provisional re-organization of the regiment we stood ready today to renew the attack on receipt of orders which it was intimated might come. But they did not come.

You might naturally think that these men had had all the aggressiveness hammered out of them—far from it! The success of their attacks has made them forget the price they paid and, tired though they are, their spirit is as indomitable as it was a week ago when they moved forward into this battle.

Late this afternoon, we were ordered relieved and now 10:10 p.m. the relieving troops are filtering in and our regiment is filtering out and back to Bois de Ogons.

It has been an awful week! Five days and six nights of steady fighting! No rest and no comfort! Wet, cold and hungry all the time! The air literally filled with shells and bullets! The very atmosphere laden with poison gas!

How have these men stood it?—I do not know.

Why have they stood it?—Because they are Americans!

We have, of course, been awfully hurt. It makes one want to cry to look at the decimated ranks of our splendid regiment. But we expected it—you remember I told you that our army was going in determined to bring about the decision before winter and that we fully realize that we should have to pay the price.

"Pour faire une omelette, il faut casser des oeufs."—The omelette is the end of this war—we are the eggs—the omelette is worth the eggs and is practically made.

Good night

Your Soldier

17 Oct 18

Dear Hugh,

When our regiment had filtered out of the position for which we had paid so dearly and left it to our successors, our Regimental PC moved back to where it was when we took off three days ago.

This morning was another dark rainy one and, under cover of the mist, we drew the regiment back from Bois de Ogons where the companies had assembled to the Bois de Beuge between Nantillois and Cierges.

There the task of untangling the companies and of restoring the permanent regimental organization was immediately commenced.

Our losses on the withdrawal were almost entirely due to shell fire and were not heavy and in our new place the shelter camp was pitched in the woods on the reverse slope of a hill where we had considerable protection.

Nevertheless, since the Boche occasionally dropped a shell in where we were and since he might at any moment open up a heavy bombardment, the men were put to digging shelters for themselves before they were allowed to rest.

The reaction had come and they were so tired that, had they not been forced to provide protection for themselves, they would have laid right down in the mud and gone to sleep regardless of shelling. During the forenoon the rolling kitchens came up and this evening the men have their stomachs full of good, warm food—the first they have had in a week—and fires having been authorized, they are warm and dry.

It has been a hard day for the few officers that remain. They have had to look after their men when, they, themselves, are even worse played out.

At Regimental Headquarters, the Colonel and the majors have been at work on the re-organization and the reports. This has been most difficult for accurate data cannot be gotten. Few of the company commanders who led the companies into the battle have come out with them and most of the first sergeants are also gone. The rolls of most of the companies are missing and even when they are available they do not show who are left in the organization.

When we arrived here, the company commanders were directed to check up "present and absent" and to try to determine their casualties by inquiry among the men.

This is given a basis for estimate but is, of course, not reliable. Many of the men who were killed or wounded were not seen when they fell. Many who were absent are neither killed nor wounded but are lost in the woods, mixed in with other troops, or are lying exhausted in shell holes.

The checks showed that about 400 men returned here with us but others are coming back all the time.

When the officers assembled this afternoon, it was a pitiful little gathering—There was no major. Only four of the seventeen captains. But a remnant of the former big bunch of lieutenants.

Do you remember that we received 18 lieutenants in the replacements at Bois des Esnes on October 10—15 of that 18 are casualties.

One of the battalions is commanded by a captain who is the only captain left in it. Another is commanded by a first lieutenant. Another is commanded by a second lieutenant.

Four of the companies are commanded by sergeants, having each lost its seven officers, and one is commanded by a corporal, having lost all its officers and all its sergeants.

All of the battalion adjutants, all of the battalion intelligence officers and all of the scout officers were killed or wounded. Only three of the seven surgeons remain.

Two of the three chaplains are casualties also. The regimental staff now consists of two officers.

By some miracle, neither the Colonel nor the Lieutenant Colonel were hurt though both of them had their helmets smashed by shrapnel balls.

We have no information as to what is next—we will re-organize as rapidly as possible and hope to receive replacements and go in again. A few days of rest will make us as good as new and we will be "in at the death."

The Boche is whipped—it only remains to cross the Meuse and clean up the job.

Good night

Your Soldier

The letter of October 17, 1918, was the last written by the Little Lead Soldier from the front. On that day, General Pershing, the chef in charge of making the omelette, wrote to General Liggett, commander of the newly created First American Army, stating, in part: "Now that Germany and the Central Powers are losing, they are begging for an armistice. . . . That is the best of reasons for our pushing the war more vigorously at this moment. . . . There can be no conclusion to this war until Germany is brought to her knees."[2]

The Little Lead Soldier did not write what happened to the Colonel, and whatever correspondence he may have had with his wife Ida cannot be found. His personal military notebook shows that he relinquished command of the 61st Infantry on October 19 and was ordered to undergo physical examination and treatment. The previous day General Hanson Ely had replaced General John McMahon as commander of the 5th Division.[3]

FOURTEEN

AFTERMATH

THE KILLING CONTINUED. BY THE END OF OCTOBER, Ludendorff had resigned and the German navy had mutinied, but the killing continued. Civil strife was everywhere in Germany. On November 10 the Kaiser abdicated, and the following day an armistice was finally signed and the bloodshed which had gone on until the last moment finally ceased.

For the Colonel, the war had ended October 19, when he was relegated to general command duty in Paris. After a respite of two weeks, the Little Lead Soldier wrote again of the exploits of the 61st Infantry, but in generalities, not with the detail that had come with actually being in the dispatch bag on the front. Apparently, the Colonel did not want to leave the end of the story untold, and to the teller belongs the tale. The tale that I am telling does not need much of those last letters. What was left of the 61st Infantry, no doubt reinforced, rebuilt, or reorganized, fought forward and crossed the Meuse River. It was ready to attack again on November 11 when news of the armistice arrived.

The Little Lead Soldier's final words of November 11, after which he retired to a small box from which he occasionally emerges, are as follows, in the emotions of the time:

The job is done (Hukins) – the wolf's fangs are pulled!

His satanic majesty, the Kaiser, is gone and the Hun empire is broken and torn.

Marshall Foch, the greatest soldier and the greatest statesman in the world, has drawn the terms of the armistice so the Boche cannot renew the fight.

Civilization has maintained itself, Christianity still rules the world, and thank God your regiment has been permitted to do its share.

Good Bye,

Your Soldier

The Colonel and Ida retired to Princeton, New Jersey. He did not mope, but took up deep sea shark fishing with rod and reel and wrote a book about it.[1] Pearl Harbor was attacked on December 7, 1941. Hugh D. Wise died in May 1942, and Ida, fifteen years later. Their three boys grew up and fought in World War II, which some historians consider to be just another phase of World War I. Richard graduated from West Point and flew with the air force. Following ROTC at Princeton University, Hugh Jr., served as a wartime colonel in counterintelligence. John served as a doctor. They all survived that war: Richard eventually retired as a colonel, Hugh Jr. practiced law in Princeton, and John was a surgeon in Trenton. They are all gone now, but the Little Lead Soldier and his tale endure.

CHRONOLOGY

October 10, 1871	Hugh D. Wise born Richmond, VA.
1898	Spanish-American War.
June 28, 1914	Archduke Franz Ferdinand of Austria assassinated in Sarajevo.
August 4, 1914	Germany invades Belgium; start of World War I.
April 6, 1917	United States declares war on Germany.
1918 March 26	Marshal Foch of France appointed Supreme Commander of Allied Forces.
April 7	61st Infantry leaves Fort Greene.
April 28	61st Infantry arrives in Brest.
May 2	Abbeville Agreement. 61st Infantry begins training at Bligny (Bar-sur-Aube).
May 27	Germans attack Chemin des Dames.
June 2–10	61st Infantry in training at Gérardmer.
June 9–14	German attack at Mondidier fails.
June 11–July 2	61st Infantry in Violu and La Cude subsectors, near La Croix-aux-Mines in Vosges.
June 21	61st Infantry "longest day" battle at Violu.
July 2–14	61st Infantry at Arches-Archettes for rest and training.
July 14–August 23	61st Infantry on front at Moyenmoutier in Vosges.

July 15–24	Germans fail at Second Battle of the Marne.
July 24	Allies agree to establish American army.
August 8	British defeat Germans at Amiens.
August 14	Germany decides to put out peace feelers.
August 23–26	61st Infantry marches to Raon-aux-Bois (Arches area).
August 24	St. Mihiel attack plan drawn up by Foch and U.S. general John J. Pershing.
August 27	Colonel relieved of command and starts to Chaumont.
	61st Infantry starts for Haussonville.
August 29	Colonel receives orders of reinstatement.
August 29–September 6	61st Infantry in training at Haussonville.
August 30	Foch has new plan for St. Mihiel.
	St. Mihiel sector turned over to Americans.
	Bobbies (police patrolmen) strike in Britain.
	Colonel resumes command.
September 6–10	61st Infantry marching to X (St. Mihiel sector).
September 12–16	St. Mihiel battle.
September 18–27	61st Infantry in rest/training in Manoncourt area.
September 26–30	American initial attack at Meuse-Argonne. Attack shut down, September 30.
September 28	General Erich Ludendorff, commander of German forces, has fit.
	Bulgaria asks for peace.
September 28–October 3	61st Infantry in rest/training at Domgermain in Toul Sector.
September 29	Clémenceau wants Pershing fired.
October 4	Americans resume attack.
	Austria-Hungary asks for peace.
October 4–5	61st Infantry treks by camion to Nixéville (Meuse-Argonne).
October 5–10	61st Infantry waits in Nixéville area.
October 6	Germans propose peace.
October 8	Americans request clarification of German peace proposal.

October 11–18	61st Infantry in Meuse-Argonne battle.
October 14	Wilson states that armistice terms are up to military leaders.
October 19	Colonel relinquishes command.
November 11	Armistice.
December 7, 1941	Pearl Harbor.
May 2, 1942	Colonel Hugh Wise dies.

GLOSSARY

abri—French for house with protection against shelling
adjutant—administrative assistant
AEF—American Expeditionary Force (American army)
archies—anti-aircraft guns
avion—French for airplane
battalion—part of a regiment
bengalore—tin gutter pipe filled with explosives
billet—lodging
Boche—derogatory slang for a German
boyaux—French for communication trenches
Brial—command post near La Croix-aux-Mines in Vosges
brigade—part of a division, consisting of 3 regiments
camion—French for truck
caserne—French for barracks
cooties—body lice
corps—a grouping of three or more regiments
C.R.—center of resistance in troop line
Croix de Guerre (cross of war)—French military honor medal
division—a grouping of three brigades
enfilade—weapon fire from the flank
Fritz—slang for Germans
G.C.—combat group
H.E.—high explosive shells
Heinie—derogatory slang for a German
H hour—hour of attack
Hqrs—headquarters
Hun—slang for German
Jean-Pierre—an observation point in the Vosges
Korman—an observation point in the Vosges
La Cude—part of the battle line near La Croix-aux-Mines
Mère Henry—mountain in Vosges, also an observation point
Minnies (minenwerefer shells)—grenades

On les aura—French rallying call, "We will get them"

OP—observation point

PC—command post

Pickelhaube—German military helmet

Poilu—French soldier

Pour faire une omelette, il faut casser des oeufs—French saying, "to make an omelette, one must break some eggs"

QM—quarter master, personnel responsible for supplies

Ranking of officers from lowest—lieutenant; captain; major; lieutenant colonel; colonel; general

regiment—a grouping of three battalions

Salome—an observation point in the Vosges

Stokes—name that the Colonel gave to an officer who commanded a Stokes Mortar group

Stokes Mortar—a type of mobile mortar launcher developed by the British

Violu—part of the battle line near La Croix-aux-Mines

Whippet—small French tank

NOTES

CHAPTER 1: THE TRAIN NORTH
1. Mead, 38, 39.
2. Goodwin, 732–34; Dos Passos, 70, 211.
3. Dos Passos, 216–19; Kennedy, 144–49.
4. Letter from Roosevelt to Wise, May 25, 1917, private collection, Hugh D. Wise, III.
5. Simpson, 253. Simpson's biography of Henry A. Wise provides the most thorough treatment of the political life of this complex man.
6. Davis, 463. Davis's article provides insight into the life of John S. Wise, as does his introduction to *The End of an Era*, authored by John S. Wise (New York: Thomas Yoselof, 1965).
7. John S. Wise, 299. The leading role that the Colonel's father played in the Battle of New Market is dramatized in the prize-winning film *Field of Lost Shoes*, produced by Thomas F. Farrell II and David M. Kennedy, directed by Sean McNamara, and the official novelization of that film by David M. Kennedy with Louise Parsley and John Rixey Moore, bearing the same title, published by Field of Lost Shoes, LLC.
8. As a lawyer and politician, Henry A. Wise authored many writings which are noted by Simpson. He also was the author of the book *Seven Decades of the Union* (Philadelphia: Lippincott, 1872). John S. Wise was the author of several books, the most notable of which was *The End of an Era* (Boston: Houghton, Mifflin, 1899). He also authored *Recollections of Thirteen Presidents* (New York: Doubleday, Page, 1906) and *Diomed: The Life, Travels and Observations of a Dog* (New York: Macmillan, 1906).
9. The Colonel's experiments with kites are described in James Wagenvoord, *Flying Kites* (New York: Macmillan, 1968), 58–66, and by articles that the Colonel wrote including "Flying in the Beginning," *Scientific American* (September, October 1932). His invention of a type of bayonet is described in Donald J. Hartman, *The U.S. Krag Bayonets* (Springfield, NJ: D & D Blade Research, 2008), 188–214.

CHAPTER 2: THE DEADLY SEAS
1. Hochschild, 216.
2. Mead, 6.
3. Ibid., 7.

4. Stone, 119, 20.
5. Mead, 117.
6. Nenninger, 116.
7. Mead, 13.
8. Ibid., 117.
9. Nenninger, 116.
10. Tuchman, 123.
11. Ibid., 172.
12. Mead, 6.
13. Bullard, 32–37.
14. Ibid., 36.
15. Mead, 143.
16. Ibid., 144.
17. Ibid., 145.
18. National Archives, USS *Pocahontas,* log book entries, April 16–28, 1918.

CHAPTER 3: WHY?

1. Tuchman, 113.
2. Kennedy, 24.
3. Tuchman, 25–27.
4. Hochschild, 188.
5. Ibid., 189.
6. Dos Passos, 40.
7. Hochschild, 314.
8. Kennedy, 73.
9. Bullard, 119.
10. Ibid., 118–20.

CHAPTER 4: AMALGAMATION

1. Pershing, 1: 33.
2. Wiest, 198–201.
3. Pershing, 1: 153.
4. Nenninger, 126.
5. Mead, 116.
6. Dos Passos, 162–64.
7. Bullard, 42.
8. Ibid., 46, 47.
9. Mead, 112.
10. Pershing, 1: 33, 34.
11. Persico, 222.
12. Dos Passos, 320–1.
13. Lloyd, 22.
14. Persico, 221–2.
15. Dos Passos, 321.

16. Mead, 101.
17. Dos Passos, 288–90.
18. Bullard, 154.
19. Dos Passos, 289.
20. Bullard, 155.
21. Dos Passos, 289.
22. Lloyd, 23.
23. Warner, 10.
24. Ibid. 12.
25. Hochschild, 180.
26. Lloyd, 22.
27. Mead, 133–41.
28. Pershing, 1: 355.
29. Stevenson, 336.
30. Pershing, 1: 365.
31. Ibid., 362.
32. Ibid., 367.
33. Stevenson, 337.
34. Pershing, 2: 28.
35. Foch, 308–9.
36. Pershing, 2: 33.
37. Pershing, 1: 265.
38. Stone, 169.
39. Bullard, 196–99.
40. Pershing, 2: 62, 3.
41. Stevenson, 359.

CHAPTER 5: THE VOSGES, THE NOT-SO-QUIET SECTOR
1. Pershing, 2: 115–16.
2. Bullard, 115.
3. Lloyd, 200, 1.

CHAPTER 7: IGNORED BY BLACK JACK
1. Pershing, 2: 114.
2. Ibid., 113.
3. Barnett, 271.
4. Pershing, 2: 92.
5. Keegan, 408.
6. Ibid.
7. Ibid., 408–9.
8. Pershing, 2: 78–79.
9. Mead, 143–46.
10. Pershing, 2: 123.
11. Ibid., 124.
12. Stone, 170.

13. Keegan, 409.
14. Barnett, 338.

CHAPTER 8: STIR IT UP
1. Pershing, 2: 172.
2. Ibid., 175.
3. Persico, 305.
4. Ibid., 303–5.

CHAPTER 10: AT LAST, A SEPARATE AMERICAN ARMY
1. Persico, 264.
2. Idem.
3. Stevenson, 348.
4. Goodspeed, 207.
5. Persico, 271.
6. Hochschild, 209.
7. Ibid., 210.
8. Stevenson, 349–50.
9. Pershing, 2: 217.
10. Dos Passos, 250, 1; Lloyd, 136; Pershing, 2: 144.
11. Pershing, 2: 238.
12. Ibid., 243.
13. Ibid., 246.
14. Idem.
15. Ibid., 247.
16. Ibid., 247–50.
17. Foch, 399–401.

CHAPTER 11: ST. MIHIEL
1. Dos Passos, 405–6.
2. Mead, 285, 294; Stevenson, 349; Marshall, 428.
3. Marshall, 422.
4. Persico, 275.
5. Mead, 296.
6. Marshall, 428.
7. Mead, 296.
8. Pershing, 2: 271.
9. Mead, 297.
10. Ibid.
11. Stevenson, 349.
12. Bullard, 286–87.

CHAPTER 12: MEUSE-ARGONNE
1. Pershing, 2: 254–55.
2. Mead, 301.
3. Lloyd, 152.

4. Mead, 300.
5. Nenninger, 150.
6. Bullard, 271.
7. Lloyd, 153.
8. Mead, 303–5.
9. Lloyd, 165.
10. Pershing, 2: 307.
11. Foch, 412.
12. Ibid., 434.
13. Marshall, 438–39.
14. Stevenson, 381.
15. Ibid., 381–83.
16. Foch, 451; Pershing, 2: 342.
17. Horne, 364.
18. Stevenson, 384; Pershing, 2: 342–43.
19. Pershing, 2: 343.

CHAPTER 13: DEBACLE
1. Pershing, 2: 344.
2. Pershing, 2: 350–51.
3. Ibid., 352.

CHAPTER 14: AFTERMATH
1. Colonel Hugh D. Wise, *Tigers of the Sea* (New York: Derrydale Press, 1937).

BIBLIOGRAPHY

Barnett, Correlli. *The Swordbearers*. London: Eyre & Spottiswoode, 1963.

Bullard, Robert Lee. *Personalities and Reminiscences of the War*. Garden City, NY: Doubleday, Page, 1925.

Davis, Curtis Carroll. "Very Well-Rounded Republican, The Several Lives of John S. Wise," *Virginia Magazine of History and Biography*, 71, no. 4, Oct. 1963, Richmond.

Dos Passos, John. *Mr. Wilson's War*. Garden City, NY: Doubleday, 1962.

Foch, Ferdinand. *The Memoirs of Marshal Foch*, translated by T. Bentley Mott. London: Doubleday Doran, 1931.

Goodspeed, D.J. *Ludendorff*. London: Rupert Hart-Davis, 1966.

Goodwin, Doris Kearns. *The Bully Pulpit*. New York: Simon & Schuster, 2014.

Hartman, Donald J. *The U.S. Krag Bayonets*. Springfield, NJ: D & D Blade Research, 2008.

Hochschild, Adam. *To End All Wars*. New York: Houghton Mifflin Harcourt, 2011.

Horne, Charles, ed. *Source Records of The Great War*, Vol. 6, National Alumni, U.S.A., 1923.

Keegan, John. *The First World War*. New York: Vintage Books, 2000.

Kennedy, David M. *Over Here: The First World War and American Society*, 25th anniversary edition. New York: Oxford University Press, 2004.

Lloyd, Nick. *Hundred Days: The Campaign that Ended World War I*. New York: Basic Books, 2014.

Marshall, S.L.A. *World War I*. New York: First Mariner Books, Houghton Mifflin, 2001.

Mead, Gary. *The Doughboys*. Woodstock, NY: Overlook Press, 2000.

Nenninger, Timothy. "American Military Effectiveness in the First World War," in *Military Effectiveness,* edited by Allan Millett and Williamson Murray, new edition. New York: Cambridge University Press, 2012.

Pershing, John. *My Experiences in the World War.* New York: Frederick A. Stokes, 1931.

Persico, Joseph E. *Eleventh Month, Eleventh Day, Eleventh Hour.* New York: Random House, 2005.

Simpson, Craig M. *A Good Southerner: The Life of Henry A. Wise of Virginia,* Chapel Hill: University of North Carolina Press, 1985.

Stevenson, David. *Cataclysm.* New York: Basic Books, 2004.

Stone, Norman. *World War One.* New York: Basic Books, 2009.

Tuchman, Barbara W. *The Zimmermann Telegram.* New York: Viking, 1958.

Wagenvoord, James. *Flying Kites.* New York: Macmillan, 1968.

Warner, Phillip. *Field-Marshal Earl Haig.* London: Bodley Head, 1991.

Wiest, Andrew. "The Reluctant Pupil, The American Army on the Western Front, 1917–18," in *World War I Companion,* edited by Matthias Strohn. Oxford, UK: Osprey, 2013.

Wise, Hugh D. "Flying in the Beginning," *Scientific American,* September, October 1932.

Wise, John S. *The End of an Era.* Boston: Houghton, Mifflin, 1899.

ACKNOWLEDGMENTS

THERE ARE MANY WHO HELPED ME IN THIS ENDEAVOR. FIRST and foremost is my wife, Mary, whose insight, honest feedback, and patience have been invaluable. It was so easy to become wrapped up in the moments of research and composing that I lost contact with reality and perspective. Mary brought me back, for which I am forever grateful. Real life is not all about war, killing, and recounting the lives of others. As a professional counselor, she reminded me of my humanity and those of others whose lives I trace. This book would not have been possible without her. Calling upon her skills as a fine artist, she was also inestimable help as a photographer. Less visibly, she also helped me as a computer researcher. In short, she has been indispensable.

Adam Hochschild has been my mentor through the many years that I have spent on this project. He encouraged me to think that my idea had merit and should be pursued. He gave me hope when I had to backtrack from paths mistakenly followed. As a professor of journalism and acclaimed author of many thoughtful and carefully researched books that I have read over the years, he opened the door for me to enter the mysterious world of authorship.

Michael Burlingame also bore with me in my travails as a first-time author. His masterful works on Abraham Lincoln ingrained in me an appreciation of the power of exhaustive research, imaginatively presented. I am grateful.

As for my grandfather who, after all, wrote most of this book, I am in awe. I have never encountered another author writing of war whose beauty of description is his equal, whether it be of people, the peaceful countryside, or the ravages of war. His opinions of that time and mine of the present day diverge. I would cherish conversing with him, but perhaps my knowledge of what has ensued would only lead to sadness. During the war my grandmother endured a previously unacknowledged and unrewarded hell. I am glad to have this opportunity to acknowledge her sacrifices.

Sue O'Donnell, editor, spent many midnight hours poring over my unfinished manuscript and making numerous needed corrections. Larry O'Donnell aided, abetted, and participated. Professional photographer Vinny Calabrese helped with photography of dated snapshots, and Linda Calabrese, herself an author, read the manuscript and provided helpful encouragement. Tony Prinster, also a Colorado attorney and first-time author, made me believe in what could be possible. Joelle McDonough scoured French bookstores searching for source materials.

I also give a tip of my hat to those of our friends who read the manuscript in its various stages and made suggestions: Doug and Annette Finnegan, Arnie and Jill Bellowe, Lois Marks and Larry Hausman, John and Peggy Polk, Jake and Jennie Aubert, Nick Mayer, Justin Aubert, and that connoisseur of fine champagne, Pierre Perignon.

I am also indebted to many authors upon whom I have relied and have cited in the bibliography. In particular I acknowledge the works of Adam Hochschild, Nick Lloyd, David M. Kennedy, Gary Mead, and Joseph Persico.

Finally, but not last, I thank Bruce H. Franklin of Westholme Publishing, copy editor Noreen O'Connor, cartographer Tracy Dungan.

INDEX